FREEDOM CITY

The sun rises on the *land* at Freedom City, Mississippi.

BRUCE HILTON

LEON HOWELL

FREEDOM CITY

The Substance of Things Hoped For

JOHN KNOX PRESS
Richmond, Virginia

Standard Book Number: 8042-0820-4
Library of Congress Catalog Card Number: 69-12340
© M. E. Bratcher 1969
Printed in the United States of America

DEDICATION

TO BARBARA

Contents

"The reason that we Negroes in Mississippi are not bitter is because most of us were brought up in the church from an early age. A child has to be taught to hate. We were taught to love and to have faith. My father used to read a scripture from the Bible: 'Faith is the substance of things hoped for and the evidence of things not seen.' "

Fannie Lou Hamer[1]

"I have one great fear in my heart, that one day when they turn to loving they will find we are turned to hating."

Words of an African in *Cry, the Beloved Country*[2]

Introduction

THIS BOOK is about a small group of people who make up a hopeful new community and how they got where they are. It includes some reflections upon the involvement of the churches in the journey of the poor *peoples* to Freedom City, but that comes after the people tell their own story.

Community organizer Saul Alinsky, a secular man, states that the church, in spite of lethargy in many aspects of its life, is "less compromised" than most other organizations; its gospel makes even the most comfortable congregations uneasy when they do not respond to the poor.

The Delta Ministry of the National Council of Churches found its mission to be precisely with the poor and dispossessed of Mississippi's Delta. This Ministry is rich ground for study itself, but that is essentially another story and will be told by other people. Bruce Hilton, who was on the DM staff for more than two years, begins the task in his new book, *The Delta Ministry*.

The churches made a commitment when they came into the Delta through the Ministry; they promised to stay until changes began to take place in the lives of those cut off from real hope. This pledge now constitutes a challenge. Because the church suffers from faddism—as do other institutions—many will be watching closely to see if it will fulfill its covenant with the poor blacks of Mississippi by continuing to fund an often controversial ministry after time passes and other issues grab newspaper headlines.

But there is no denying the need of the people who are in fact the ministry. If the American church cannot bring hope, yes, but far more tangible changes into the lives of its own countrymen, there appears almost no possibility that it can begin to tackle the even more complex tasks of responsible usage of our great resources in a world which is filled with human beings who are hungry and captive and diseased.

The "wretched of the earth," at home and abroad, will be awaiting an answer.

There are many people to whom anyone who has worked on a subject as absorbing as Freedom City would wish to express appreciation. But there are limits of space, and one would thank at least a few individuals.

Mr. Wayne Cowan, editor of *Christianity and Crisis,* first suggested that I write about the DM. Hints of the two articles which resulted from that first effort and appeared in *Christianity and Crisis* will be found in this book.

Individuals with the Delta Ministry staff in Mississippi—Rev. Arthur Thomas, Mr. Owen Brooks, Mr. Bruce Hilton, Mrs. Thelma Barnes, Rev. Roger Smith, Miss Sue Geiger, and Rev. Rims Barber —have patiently endured my continuing questions and inquiries. Dr. Jon Regier, Dr. Henry McCanna, Dr. Colin Williams, Mrs. Karen Barracuda, and especially Rev. Bruce Hanson, all of whom have had responsibilities in New York for meeting continual financial crises and fighting off bureaucratic strangulation of the Ministry, have been constantly helpful. Miss Beryl Ramsay, both as New York secretary for the DM and through her excellent B.D. thesis on the Ministry, made the work go easier.

I am grateful to my colleagues in the University Christian Movement for their patience when deadlines created extra work for them.

Through their actions my parents taught me much about what it means to care selflessly for other people. My wife, Barbara, a skillful writer, has been a tolerant and helpful critic of the less precise efforts of her husband. She relieved me of much of the onerous task of typing the final manuscript. Most praiseworthy, she —along with Gail and Leah—endured, with affection, too many days with a distracted man.

But, in the final analysis, there would be no reason for these words at all if it had not been for the courage and faith of the citizens of Freedom City; to them I owe the greatest debt of all.

FREEDOM CITY

MISSISSIPPI

SOME PLACES, like some people, need no introduction. Mississippi has burned its way into the national consciousness over the past few years; everyone has an opinion and finds it as easy to condemn Mississippi as it is difficult to work toward change in that apostate state.

One could hurl harsh words in an angry stream and find it difficult to miss so obvious a mark. David Halberstam was once accused by Poland of libel in his writings. His laconic reply, "It is impossible to libel Poland," could equally be applied to Mississippi.

If Mississippi under Gov. James Coleman appeared to most of the nation rather sedate in the late 1950's and if "Ole" Ross Barnett came across more the hapless buffoon (the Lester Maddox of the early '60's) than the dangerous tyrant, the vicious reality of life in the Magnolia State revealed by the 1964 Mississippi Summer Project jolted the nation.

The terrible deaths of the three civil rights workers in Philadelphia (City of Brotherly Love), Mississippi, and the countless beatings, church burnings, and acts of terrorism against the workers and black people of Mississippi involved in that "long hot summer," all fully recorded by the national news media, demonstrated to America what Negroes in Mississippi had known all along to be the price of breaking the rules of the "closed society."

Mr. Hodding Carter, III, urbane editor of the *Delta Democrat Times*, commented in the introduction of the *Mississippi Black Paper:* "There will be many Mississippians, thoroughly respectable men and women, who will try to forget that events such as those described in these pages ever occurred, or to pretend that they did not. If it does nothing else, this book should provide an effective antidote to that hypocrisy and a vivid reminder to all Americans that the old truism is still valid: 'All that is necessary for the triumph of evil is for good men to do nothing.' It took a summer of shame for us in Mississippi to appreciate this warning."[1]

Things settled down somewhat that winter and the nation's

attention was diverted to Vietnam and the fires which began to spring up out of the big city ghettos; there was a general feeling that things were a little better in Mississippi. But that long-running drama, "Man's Inhumanity to Man," is played on many stages at many times. The cast of characters in the Mississippi version, however, demands attention time and again as the scenario alters while the theme stays the same.

On June 6, 1966, James Meredith, that most singular man, was shot down like a "goddam rabbit" near Hernando while marching against fear. Once again the jolt of awareness focused attention on the aberrations of the Magnolia State.

In the late spring of 1967, Mississippi was again singled out as this country found, to its continued shame, that an incredible number of its own people, jobless, homeless, and sick, were also severely undernourished and, indeed, starving.

The disgraceful slaying of Martin Luther King, Jr., in Memphis, Tennessee, April 4, 1968, symbolized our national sickness; but that it took place in Memphis once again pointed out that the hard realities of the Delta are something other than its own myths.

In short, if one were writing about many other parts of the world, it would be important to set the stage in considerably more detail. In the brief compass of this book, it is not necessary to review extensively what is known. A few brief observations should suffice to remind us of the problems of the state and its alienation from the rest of the country. (Where 87 percent voted for Goldwater in the 1964 election while the rest of the South went 52-48 percent for Johnson; where Kennedy half-dollars once sold for twenty-five cents in a corny demonstration that that was all they were worth.)

In a poetic description of the context for that great source of Mississippi pride, Ole Miss football, *Sports Illustrated*, in 1967, gushed:

> There are two things that a man can depend on down in Itta Bena or Yazoo City, where the heritage is Faulkner and life can be either magnolia sweet or red-dust sour. He knows if his daughter is beautiful he will send her off to Mississippi —Ole Miss, it has to be called—and have her sing Girl Scout songs on the sorority-house steps and try to grow up to be Miss

America, as two Ole Misses have in the past eight years. And if his son has a broad back and a strong heart he will send him to Ole Miss, too, to let him work under Johnny Vaught and join a winning football team. As a result, there is not an autumn spectacle in the whole state of Mississippi that can rival what Ole Miss offers—its potential Miss Americas and its victorious football weekends.[2]

The Right Rev. Edward J. Pendergrass, Methodist Bishop of Mississippi, once attacked the Delta Ministry by charging: "It is not ecumenical in nature. The program does not involve church people in Mississippi."[3]

One might wish for better both from the only literate sports magazine in the country and perhaps, even, from a Methodist bishop. Both forget about the black man. The Negro. Which is true of the way things have been in Mississippi as well as in the nation, but not of the way things ought to be. For it was the black man, who, in the words thirty-three years ago of David Cohn, an unusually perceptive native of the Delta: ". . . brought order out of primeval wilderness, felling the trees, digging the ditches and draining the swamps. . . . Wherever one looks in this land, whatever one sees that is the work of man, was created by the toiling, straining bodies of the blacks."[4]

Even though Ole Miss's football fortunes have waned in recent years and she could use some of her native black talent which now sparks Big Ten teams, none plays for Johnny Vaught; no black girls are going to be Miss Mississippi for a few eons yet. But, one would hasten to add, Negro churchmen are indeed involved in the Delta Ministry. One native says flatly that ninety percent of the Negro people in Mississippi have gone to church all their lives.

Allen Thompson, mayor of Jackson for twenty years, cannot be accused of overlooking the blacks in his midst. He has the distinction of being the pacesetter for the nation in the use of an anti-personnel "tank" to keep them in their place as early as 1964. But he has his own tunnel vision. In the spring of 1968 he vehemently denied that there were slums in Jackson. He seemed surprised to find that, in fact, there might be one or two after he was taken on a visit by Negro leaders.

All of which is by way of illustration: it is easy to overlook what we don't want to see. What there is to see in Mississippi gives the lie to much of what we have assumed about our own country. In stark intensity, it reveals more than we would wish to know about our own sickness.

But one certainty emerges; the agonies of our cities, the crises which literally can rip this nation apart, will not so easily be ignored. Our unconcern for the systematic destruction of human beings in Mississippi and other parts of the South has come back to haunt us as the portent of our national destruction. It is America's failure; it is only most easily detected in the Mississippi Delta.

The Delta, shrouded in myth, refers specifically to that portion of the level, rich "black-belt" stretching from Virginia into Arkansas, which runs through the northwestern corner of Mississippi. It is, more precisely, the flat alluvial plain, with topsoil thirty-five feet deep in places, which runs 200 miles long and about sixty-five miles wide; it is defined by the two major river systems almost surrounding it, the lower Mississippi and the Coldwater-Tallahatchie-Yazoo. Created by countless floods, the six million acres contain some of the richest land in America.

William Faulkner wrote once that cotton there "grows man-tall in the very cracks of the sidewalk." Cotton has been king here and remains so; but the fragile fiber has often been a cantankerous despot. Ironically an outsider—an Egyptian intruder—it has made dictatorial demands on the organizaton of life. Delicate and demanding, cotton requires constant protection from beetles and weeds; water causes it to rot and a drought burns it out. The soil which nourishes it is soon exhausted. But the Mississippi planter has, with the great assistance of his much cursed national government, turned on his tyrant, and, if he is not in complete control, he has worked out something of an entente. Mechanical pickers, long unattractive to the planter (in 1953 only fourteen percent of the Delta's crop was picked by machine), have almost completely taken over the role of the human picker. As much as ninety-five percent of the 1967 crop was machine picked.

Chemicals, in large part developed with federal funds, likewise have replaced the cotton chopper. Improved fertilizers, new cultivation theories, and the increased efficiency of the machines have more than doubled the yield per acre. Man hours per acre once averaged 165 for men and mules; last year machines cut that to thirty-five, and it is dropping.

There have been two results. In large part because of federal pressure to reduce the amount of land planted, less than half the 2,554,000 acres cultivated in 1953 were needed fifteen years later to produce more cotton. And in 1966, the government not only paid people not to grow cotton but had bought enough of what was produced to have a surplus of more than 14,000,000 bales.

Also, there is no longer any need for the seasonal worker. Over the past decade, more than 100,000 people have been thrown out of work, such as it was.

The calumny of America stands exposed to itself and the world in these statistics. For the federal government not only produced most of the momentum for the technological advances which started the revolution in the Delta, it also has worked very skillfully to protect the growers affected by it. We have, that is, a federal "welfare" program for the wealthy plantation owner. But the federal government has done nothing significant at all for the people affected by this revolution, and the state of Mississippi has done even less.

What little that gets done through anti-poverty programs remains almost exclusively in the hands of those who use it to manipulate and manage the lives of those they are supposedly helping. And in the midst of it all, people have the gall to spout hackneyed phrases about "I got what I got on my own. They could too if they weren't sorry."

Item: The anti-poverty program in Clarksdale received about two million dollars last year. Half the members of its twenty-eight-member board, all white conservatives, quit, complaining that too much money was being wasted and that the government was attempting to make a spectacle out of them. Twenty-seven farming units in the same county received two million dollars, the same figure almost exactly, not to plant cotton. If there were complaints about federal wastefulness, no one has recorded them.

The result over the past few years, as surely all know by now, has been a flood of "refugees" out of the state and along the bus routes, highways, and rail lines to St. Louis and Chicago and other points north. (One million from Mississippi in Chicago alone.) The result has been to pour the fuel of discontent and brokenness onto the already volatile and overcrowded ghettos, suffering their own deprivation.

Overwhelming evidence confirms that official Mississippi views this exodus as its own "final solution," though it vehemently denies it for the record. Yet the primary reason for keeping industry out of the Delta has been precisely this. In an interview on Public Broadcasting Laboratory, Mr. Sims Lockett, a Clarksdale lawyer who speaks for the conservatives in Mississippi, said:

> I don't think that there is any true future for the Negro in this community or the white persons in this community . . . unless and until we change the racial ratio.
> If we had—if half the Negroes in this community left tomorrow, the ones that are left behind would benefit immensely . . . We've got to distribute the Negroes more evenly throughout the country. I do not think that the cities can survive where the Negroes become dominant insofar as numbers are concerned. Nor do I think that the South can survive if we continue with the ratio that we have at the present time.[5]

In other words, we in Mississippi wash our hands of it all; we can't worry about people we no longer need.

This bit of casuistry simply won't do it, not for a country which claims to have a social conscience, especially not for a people that identifies itself as Christian.

One historical example should be an adequate illustration of why such a position is intolerable.

There were 189,884 Negro registered voters in Mississippi in 1890, one of the least-known facts of Mississippi history. Mississippi was conditionally readmitted to the Union in 1870; one of the specifications was that it would never "amend or change [the Constitution of Mississippi of 1869] as to deprive any citizen or class of citizens of the United States of the right to vote who are entitled to vote by the constitution herein recognized." The Constitution of 1869 said that the right to vote went to all male inhabitants twenty-one or over who had resided in Mississippi for six months and were not insane. From 1890, when there were 70,000 more registered Negro voters than white, intense pressure and discrimination reduced that number to 23,801 in 1961.[6]

There are those who contend that the endemic violence of Mississippi over the past eighty years springs precisely from this massive drive for disenfranchisement. That, certainly, was the ingredient which set off the chain of horror of the summer of 1964.

Professor James W. Silver, in his brilliant exploration of the double captivity of black and white in Mississippi in *Mississippi: The Closed Society* (must reading for any real understanding of Mississippi), states:

> Violence and the threat of violence have confirmed and enforced the image of unanimity.
> This, then, is the essence of the closed society. For whatever reason, the community sets up the orthodox view. Its people are constantly indoctrinated. . . . When there is no effective challenge to the code, a mild toleration of dissent is evident, provided the non-conformist is tactful and does not go far. But with a substantial challenge from the outside—to slavery in the 1850's and to segregation in the 1950's—the society tightly closes its ranks, becomes inflexible and stubborn, and lets no scruple, legal or ethical, stand in the way of the enforcement of the orthodoxy. The voice of reason is stilled and the moderate either goes along or is eliminated.

A whole people has been systematically disenfranchised, exploited, deprived, manipulated, and broken, in the name of the orthodoxy and for the sake of the needs of the cotton-dominated economy. And now these destroyed people, no longer needed, increasingly a burden and a growing threat to the unanimity of the society, and, indeed, to the physical safety of its people, will be turned loose to exist in desperate poverty or to journey to a new location, unprepared, lost, and vulnerable. Violence, direct and indirect, has driven them from their native land.

There are, of course, large numbers of moderates in Mississippi who blanch at the thought of overt violence. Yet through fear, and more precisely, through the lack of concern that grips our whole society—now severely indicted in the Kerner Commission report as "white racist"—these moderates have not moved to close off either the physical violence of the nightrider or the more subtle violence of the poverty of the lives of those they have used and discarded.

> Peckerwoods ride by and shoot into Negro shanties at night; good people refuse to distribute federal surplus food to hungry Negroes in the winter, thus insuring their eager return to the fields at $3 a day come spring (it is not unheard of for Delta Negroes to die from cold and malnutrition in the winter). It is the difference between those who, merrily sucking a jawful of Red Man tobacco, are willing to work and sweat to dig a grave in the night to hide their murder, and that smaller group whom Hodding Carter called "the uptown Ku Klux Klan"—men of substance who would not think of night riding, either to kill or to catch a killer; they are the Rotary Club of Indianola who did their civic duty by buying more riot guns for the local police when the SNCC youngsters came to town, not the farmers who later burned down the Freedom Labor Union's headquarters.[8]

As the young and able and the bright have left the state, those left behind are often the very young and the very old. Most poignant are the children. "The Negro children of Mississippi are its deepest tragedy. Beyond the violence and the obvious planned manipulation of a people is the awful knowledge that here are thousands and thousands of children who will not ever be free in any real sense. They were marked in the womb, debased in infancy, and face a life already circumscribed by their stunted bodies and minds. I am chilled by that memory."

These words, spoken slowly and with difficulty by Rev. David Barnes, came from a year he spent in Mississippi as a volunteer for the Delta Ministry of the National Council of Churches. He said them a year before the terrible "hungry children report" of the Southern Regional Council. Six doctors of national reputation made a study of children in the Delta and reported:

> In sum, we saw children who are hungry and who are sick —children for whom hunger is a daily fact of life and sickness, in many forms, an inevitability. We do not want to quibble over words but "malnutrition" is not quite what we found; the boys and girls we saw were hungry—weak, in pain, sick; their lives

are being shortened; they are, in fact, visibly and predictably losing their health, their energy, their spirits. They are suffering from hunger and disease and directly or indirectly they are dying from them—which is exactly what "starvation" means.[9]

If the crime rests directly on the heads of those who have perpetuated the dehumanizing system in Mississippi, all America stands indicted for its "uptown KKK" silence. The history of federal involvement in Mississippi has been one of compromise, often in the name of political realities, with practices and conditions unconscionable for any nation, much less one which claims to be just.

It began in early days and implicates us today. One illustration will, again, serve as mirror of the whole.

In January, 1965, the remarkable Mrs. Fannie Lou Hamer contested the right of Representative Jamie L. Whitten to represent the Second Congressional District. Her charges were simple and direct: Whitten did not have the right to represent that district because 52.45 percent of the adult population was black but only 2.97 percent was allowed to register to vote, both because of planned intimidation and the long history cited earlier of systematic denial of the vote to Negroes. Two other women challenged their representative on the same grounds.

In Congress on January 4, 1965, all other members were sworn in to decide how to handle the challenge. Confronted with this evidence, Congress had the opportunity to refuse the seats until the case was settled; almost surely with the backing of the administration, Speaker John McCormick and Rep. Carl Albert managed to get the delegation seated until the challenge was decided (by a vote of 276-149). Rep. James Roosevelt of California had prepared a speech he was never able to deliver: "We dare not let men pretend to a seat in this honorable House who have been chosen by a closed vote in a closed society. If we do, we betray this House and the people of the United States and the Constitution they wrote for us."

After the seating of the representatives, the challenge was simply not recognized again. Political expediency at the highest levels demanded that the powerful southern bloc not be riled.[10]

Into this convoluted matrix came the national and world

church, answering a Macedonian call from black leaders in 1963. And it was with these people—the homeless refugees—that the Delta Ministry, begun September 1, 1964, started to work. What follows in this book is some attempt to record the remarkable journey of a pilgrim people, wandering in faith on a modern-day exodus. It is essentially about them and their plight that this book concerns itself, but it will also consider briefly the difficult role played by the church as it tried to stand with these *peoples* in their need. For this reason, the two will interweave, though my obvious intent is to talk more about the *peoples* as the church than the institution.

This is at best only an interim reporting of a continuing process. The task touched upon has only begun; the conditions determining the task have not seriously been addressed by the church or the nation. (I had thought at one time of calling this piece "A Single Step," referring to the Chinese saying popularized by President John F. Kennedy, "A journey of a thousand miles begins with a single step.")

The report is compiled by a white outsider who, although a native of Tennessee, finds Mississippi a different world, whose association with the ministry and the state, while extending over several years, has never been long-term.

There will be other reports, more complete, perhaps more hopeful. Plays and books and pictures and songs, written by black people like Isaac Foster, will tell far more intimately than I of what life was like in Mississippi in 1948 and 1958 and 1968, and perhaps what it has become in 1980.

Someday, one trusts, the church in Mississippi will answer the call of God's world and perform a total mission to all people and all classes. And that will be a report eagerly awaited.

In the meantime, there may be some value in the intimations urgently offered by a concerned observer, one haunted by the knowledge that in Mississippi as indeed in India and Harlem and Guatemala and on Oklahoma Indian reservations, there are people who are hungry, who are sick, who are homeless, who are imprisoned by their society; haunted by that sure knowledge that the rationalizations of the middle class—"I got where I am because I worked for it"—are completely untenable in the face of the proof we now have that a baby in the womb whose mother has a protein deficiency is already crippled, that a child starving at two will never be able to catch up physically, mentally, or emotionally; haunted by the riches of a nation that makes the building of superhighways and going to the moon priorities over feeding our hungry, releasing our captives; haunted by the pious protestations of national morality in the face of such sure evidence of our corruption; and haunted by the words of warning in the Bible that we each have a final report to make, and, whatever judgment day means in our secular age, that we must face the seering biblical warning:

> ". . . for I was hungry and you gave me no food, I was thirsty and you gave me no drink, I was a stranger and you did not welcome me, naked and you did not clothe me, sick and in prison and you did not visit me." Then they also will answer, "Lord, when did we see thee hungry or thirsty or a stranger or naked or sick or in prison, and did not minister to thee?" Then he will answer them, "Truly, I say to you, as you did it not to one of the least of these, you did it not to me." And they will go away into eternal punishment . . . (Matt. 25:42-46).

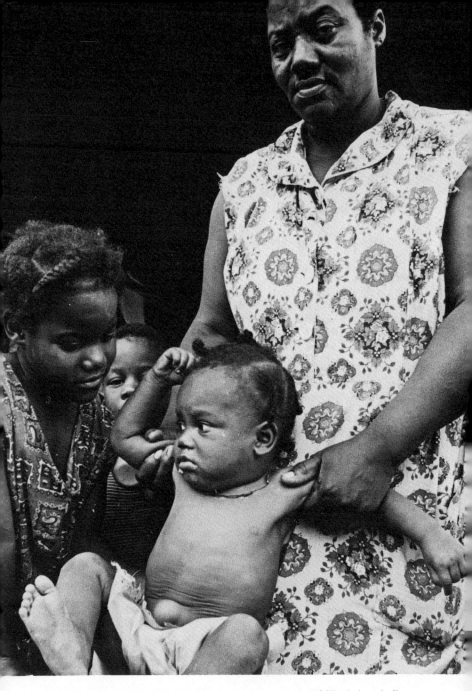

A Mississippi Delta child with the common "umbilical hernia," a tragic result of poor midwifery. In the Delta fewer than one percent of Negro mothers deliver their children in the hospital.

AL CLAYTON

THE NIGHT OF WATCHING

"And at the end of four hundred and thirty years, on that very day, all the hosts of the LORD went out from the land of Egypt. It was a night of watching by the LORD, to bring them out of the land of Egypt" (Exod. 12:41-42).

WHAT A SHAME that life on the fabulously rich land of the Mississippi Delta doesn't really correspond to its legend. For some few it always has and still does provide a life of ease; but for the vast majority, it remains a rich land of poor people.

There is a lush beauty about the Delta landscape in the growing days of spring. But winter presents another face: raw, bare, drab, oppressive. Humid winds whip across barren fields, rattling boards and penetrating the cracks of defenseless shacks. In the best of times for the poor man of Mississippi, winter constitutes a bitter struggle for simple survival. Any money saved is soon consumed by the basic ingredients of life: food, fuel, perhaps some shoes. More common is the borrowing against future work for the "man"; owing one's soul, if not to the company store, certainly to "Mr. Charlie."

But for many these are the worst of times; mechanization has made the field hand all but obsolete; scattered black militancy has infuriated some plantation owners, provided excuses for others. The loans tendered to insure hands are less frequent. Evictions pile up, as pitiful shanties are torn down or burned to make room for more productive use of the land. The result has been to increase the destitution of those who have lived by and for the land for generations.

Solutions seem impossible and hope futile. Forlorn families, broken by the land—illiterate, unskilled—huddle in dilapidated shacks, a few of which are literally antebellum (but hardly Tara). Staying alive fills the day; whatever dreams of better things which

remain almost surely center around the following of some relative
to the delights of the Chicago ghettos or the ease of East St. Louis,
poor enough stuff for the dreams of any man, much less one who
may never have been outside the state.

The winter of 1966 was especially cruel. Subfreezing temperatures grasped the Delta in an icy vise. Degrees of starvation are
hairs hard to split, but the food situation was more desperate than
ever. Ninety percent of the houses of black tenants were without
toilet or bathing facilities. The average income of the black man
in the Delta was $456 a year. Constant sickness and the enervation
of hunger drained the energy needed even for anger.

Most depressing were the conversations that filled this "long
cold winter." The Delta Council, influential voice of the planters,
estimated that mechanical cotton pickers would harvest ninety to
ninety-five percent of the cotton crop that fall; they also felt that
the 1965 Food and Fiber Act, passed in an attempt to stem the
massive cotton surpluses, would mean that as much as twenty-five
percent less cotton would be planted in 1966.

The day-labor "stars," those who drive tractors and repair
equipment, would be cut by as much as 6500 that year; this meant
about 30,000 people whose inadequate means of support would be
ended altogether. The need for choppers and pickers, those less
favored on the plantation scale, would be reduced by as much as
half, affecting at least 30,000 more people. (Over the whole state,
the total farm work force in 1960 was 280,377 but by 1965 it had
dropped below 200,000.)

Congressman Joseph Resnick of New York, who visited the
state at his own expense in November, 1965, was a lonely congressional voice (did we really expect Sen. James Eastland or Rep.
Jamie Whitten to be concerned?) writing to the Attorney General
of the United States: "In spite of the fact that this potential human
disaster is well known in Mississippi, not one single state or federal
employee or agency has made plans to cope with the extremely
unfortunate situation."[1]

The Delta Ministry, aware of the completely inadequate food
value of the food commodities program of the government, knew,
nevertheless, that for many these surplus foods would mean life.

(The commodities, often old and moldy or crawling with bugs and weevils, normally consisted of dried milk, dried beans, flour, and perhaps a little peanut butter or a can of processed meat—hardly a balanced diet.) In the winter of 1964, the Ministry, judging that only half of the 600,000 people needing food could get it, joined with the National Student Association to push the Department of Agriculture to increase the supplies.

Talk, meetings, threats, and pleas filled the winter, the spring, the summer! The only conspicuous results came in an occasional county where the shrewd bluff of the Delta Ministry was successful. It offered to make Forrest County a trial case for food distribution by the poor to the poor if the Department of Agriculture would release the commodities to it. Forrest County came up with its own program. The same thing happened in Madison County. The Delta Ministry next offered to set up distribution in any county without a program and then the state decided to set up its own program, Operation HELP. It is doubtful that the DM ever really expected to be approved as the agency or knew what it would have done had it been. But it did force, by this threat, several very reluctant counties to set up their own programs and, finally, the state acted. More accurately, the state gave the appearance that it might act.

On September 15, in answer to questions from DM, an associate to Agriculture Secretary Orvil Freeman, stated: "The OEO assistance which will soon become available will help to get food to an additional 500,000 needy in the state, and on a year-round basis."[2]

Weeks passed; nothing happened. As if to illustrate how the programs that did exist were used to manipulate the poor, the families who were living in tents at Strike City, near Greenville, were told by Washington County (often called the most progressive in the state) welfare officials that they were no longer eligible for commodities. As plantation workers, before they struck and were evicted, they had had no trouble receiving the commodities.

On November 23, however, something did happen. OEO and USDA signed a six-month contract with state officials for "Operation HELP." They promised to put it into effect within sixty days and to hire almost 500 poor people to aid in distribution.

Or had something happened? Christmas came and went and

nothing concrete seemed to develop. On January 6, 1966, Mrs. Annie Devine, well known for her work in the Freedom Democratic Party, talked with the State Welfare Director, Miss Evelyn Gandy (who had developed her humanitarian instincts as legislative assistant to that notorious racist, Sen. Theodore Bilbo).

"Mrs. Palmer and I visited about one hour with Miss Gandy, who was very friendly and answered our questions as limited and reserved as she could get away with.

"Question 1: Has the state advisory committee for Operation HELP been set up?

"Answer: No, we are so busy we really have not found time. Many county supervisors have not approved the plan . . ."[3]

In early January, Vernon Dahmer, a Negro Civil Rights leader who owned his own land, house, and small store near Hattiesburg, died; his house had been fire-bombed and he died within twenty-four hours of burns and smoke inhalation.

On January 22, snow fell for the third time in a week; the temperature hit a low of eighteen degrees.

AND NOTHING HAPPENED!

Increasingly desperate and angry people began to talk with each other; on January 24, the Freedom Democratic Party, the Mississippi Freedom Labor Union, and the Delta Ministry decided to issue a call to "all the poor people in the state," to join together to talk about finding food, homes, and jobs. (According to one Mississippi Negro, "Once more the NAACP didn't come through." It declined to join with the other three organizations in sponsoring the meeting.)

"We was all hungry, it was real bad," said Mrs. Ora Wilson, "and we was lookin' for some way out."

Seven hundred people flooded Mt. Beulah, the old school which had been reclaimed by the Delta Ministry as an integrated conference ground and training center. Long, heated discussions ensued. They decided to call themselves the "Poor Peoples Conference," and one of its first acts was to send a telegram directly to President Johnson with harsh criticism of federal programs. (The direct plea to the President reappeared as in a melancholy refrain on the Public Broadcasting Laboratory, January 7, 1968, when an old woman field hand, solid, emotional, hoe in hand, shouted out from the middle of a cotton field, "This is for the President. I would like for you to help us down here in Mississippi. We are not surviving a little bit. There are children hungry, and peoples are not gettin' a decent living! And I know it is in your power, that you can send help.")

The need to band together for effective protest was stressed; this desire had grown rapidly since the experiences of the Mississippi Summer Project of 1964. (One story made the rounds about two boys, one older and bigger than the other; as they walked down the road, the older displayed his marksmanship with stones of all sizes. Along the way he scattered dogs, birds, pigs, cows, and even ran off a horse. Suddenly the younger boy spotted a hornet's nest and urged his skilled companion to riddle it. When the wiser boy hesitated, the younger asked, "Why?" "Cause, man, they's organized.")

Word came the next day that two elderly Negroes had been discovered frozen to death in a Delta shanty. The discussion grew increasingly intense. Some asked how they could make the whole country aware of the terrible situation of Mississippi's poor. A number of ways were explored. One seemed simple enough. Burn the storehouses where the surplus but undistributed food was held. Three people visited a federal bird sanctuary and reported that the man in charge appeared very pleased at their interest in "his garden." One wonders what he would have thought had he known they were thinking of moving several hundred people into that very spot. Others suggested camping (presaging the 1968 "shanty town" in Washington, D.C.) along a major highway, to increase the visibility of the conditions of the poor.

The proposal receiving most interest involved buying some land on which to build a *new* town, a place where people could know the security of food and lodging, the dignity of work, and the freedom of running their own lives.

That prospect was not forgotten, but required too much to implement, and so the action determined upon by the group, after long debate, was a move to the Greenville Air Force Base. Mr. Isaac Foster, an organizer of the tractor drivers strike the previous spring, remembers: "Everybody there just about was willing but also most everybody was afraid. While they were hasslin' violently on whether they would do it or not, Mrs. Ida Mae Lawrence, who ain't afraid of nobody, finally broke out with, 'Dammit, I'm goin'. All of you too afraid, go home and eat some more greens.' She made the big pitch and then Mrs. Unita Blackwell (known for her work in the MFDP) came. She supported the idea, and then they wanted to know who would lead.

" 'Isaac, you've been running your mouth, why don't you be the man leader?'

" 'Okay, I'll do it. Let's go.' (Mrs. Blackwell, Mrs. Lawrence, and Mr. Foster were chosen as co-chairmen by the group.)

"We told them, 'Everybody who want to go, let's go. Everybody who don't want to go and have a place to go back to, go on back. Everybody who don't want to go and don't have a place to go back to, stay here.' So that's how the group divided up. All of them really wanted to go."

The Greenville Air Force Base, sitting on land leased to the government by the city, contains 2000 acres of carefully maintained grounds; its 300 buildings, still in good shape, yawned empty and inviting to those who had had snow filtering in on them during the week. Only the small municipal airport made any use of the air base at that time.

At 6:45 A.M., January 31, a strange entourage swept past a bewildered guard at the entry gate; cars slammed to a halt and people jumped out and dashed for the nearest building, which happened to have been, once upon a time, an officers club.

Mr. Foster recalls: "The biggest man there, after we broke the door down and got in, and this colonel came and asked us to leave or he was going to call the cops, this big man fainted. We thought he had a heart attack. Others really got sick. But they all stayed, many others joined us, and many more would have if we could have stayed longer."

The *Washington Post* wrote the next day:

> A group of Negroes invaded the deactivated Greenville Air Force Base today saying, "We are here because we are hungry and cold and we have no jobs or land."

They brought blankets and clothing—but no food—and moved into an unheated wooden building near the main gate.

Law enforcement officers ringed the area but took no action when they couldn't decide who had jurisdiction—city, county, or federal authorities. (It was a government reservation on city property out in the county.)

"We don't want charity," said the Negroes in a statement released by civil rights groups. "We are willing to work for ourselves if given a chance." They identified themselves as the Poor Peoples' Conference.

They marched through the main gate after sunrise and caught base guards by surprise. There was still snow on the ground from a record cold spell over the weekend and at mid-day temperatures remained near freezing. . . .

The Poor Peoples' statement said: "We are at the Greenville Air Force Base because it is federal property and there are hundreds of empty houses and buildings. We need those houses and the land. We could be trained for jobs in the buildings."

The statement asked President Johnson: "Whose side are you on, the poor people or the millionaires?"

It also charged that federal commodities distributed to the needy were "old and full of bugs and weevils." The Negroes asked for fresh vegetables, fruits, and meats, saying, "We want to decide what foods we want to eat."[4]

The local people and the media interpreted the "invasion" as another civil rights demonstration; in the minds of many of those involved, however, it was considerably more basic. They needed homes; the federal government, which had appeared more interested in them than the state, had 300 sitting empty. They needed food; commodities bought by the national government existed but were being held back by the state. Some even talked of how it would be if the food was flown in to them, literally over the heads of the state.

Preparations for a long stay were underway; two stoves were put into place, mattresses and quilts served as sleeping pads, and a sign appeared: "This is our home; please knock before entering." Committees formed. Other people, many of whom had first heard about the audacious move on the radio, showed up during the day. After a time, the gates were locked, but determined people climbed over or under the fence. The best estimate of the total who got in finally is one hundred.

They began to attract national attention. Said one of the participants: "Some lawyer or other flew down and asked us to send people to Washington to talk about concessions. And we said some crazy thing like, 'planes land here; you can talk to us about food here. We are staying together.' "

And that night, while they attempted to sleep, 150 Air Police, carefully selected from many different bases as far west as Denver, flew into Greenville.

By Tuesday morning at eleven the Air Force's finest had lined up outside the building. Maj. Gen. R. W. Puryear, given the onerous task of clearing the base, requested the group to leave on its own. "You have become a source of danger to government property and—I might add—to yourselves."

The general helpfully pointed out that the building, without proper sanitation or water, was a fire and health hazard. Mr. Foster replied: "This can't be your reason for wanting us out because all over Mississippi Negro homes don't have electricity or water or fire protection."

Puryear promised that the proper authorities would hear their grievances and gave them twenty minutes to decide to come out without coercion. But these people were inside the base precisely because they had grown weary of filing complaints. Soon, Mrs. Blackwell told the general, "The group unanimously voted to stay."

When the time passed, the Air Police broke a small window and unlocked the door. About thirty of the very young and very old walked out of the building while the remaining seventy or so were lugged out, individually, carried off the base, and released when they were off federal property. Several of the AP's were Negroes and the poor peoples shouted at them, "These are your own people."

Before they left, however, a federal spokesman had promised that the aid they were seeking would be sped up. Two days later OEO approved a $1.2 million grant for the Mississippi Department of Public Welfare to use in hiring hundreds of poor persons to distribute $24 million in surplus farm commodities.

The good burghers of Mississippi were outraged, of course. And thirty-one Methodist ministers there sharply criticized the involvement of the DM in the incident: ". . . we don't believe that such defiance of the law is in keeping with the stated Christian objectives of the NCC. . . . We call upon all men to seek redress of their grievances through proper channels of law and order. We recommit ourselves to work in the faith that all men who are open to love of God in Christ will find ways to establish rights, reconcile differences and heal the hurt of our society."

Criticism did not come from Mississippi alone; the Episcopal Church's Executive Council, meeting in Greenwich, Conn., passed a resolution, proposed by a man from Memphis, "deploring the entering and occupying of Federal Government property. . . . [Federal, state and local agencies were urged] to provide adequate assistance to relieve the deplorable conditions of the Delta poor which precipitated this action."[5]

The crux of the issue for many became the role of the DM in planning and carrying out the live-in. Had Rev. Art Thomas, Mr. Owen Brooks, and Rev. Warren McKenna, as DM leadership, plotted the whole thing? How could they justify breaking the law?

Part of the argument stems from a Mississippi self-deception. "Ignorant, uneducated" farm hands would not be capable of taking such action on their own; outsiders had to stir these "nigras" up— which is a pity. For really knowing an Isaac Foster or Ida Mae Lawrence or Unita Blackwell would immediately remove any doubts that they were capable of planning and carrying out this, or many other, actions.

(In the summer of 1967 I sat in the posh office of a well-to-do Delta businessman with a staff member of the Delta Ministry. A group of young Negroes had been protesting discrimination in this man's business; a major boycott was in the offing. The businessman had asked for a few days to make some adjustments, which included transferring an intransigent manager; he had received the time and made the concessions demanded. The owner told the staff member he wanted to give him a small gift for helping to gain time for the changes. To his amazement, the envelope contained five twenty-dollar bills. His first reaction was to give the "bribe" back but after pointing out to the man that he had only been liaison for the whole event his face lit up. "I'll tell you what. We'll take this as a contribution to buy food stamps for poor people." After we left, he said, "That man simply can't believe that any black kids could do what they did on their own. He gave me this to help him out if any rough spots turn up." The next day, on official stationery, the DM sent a letter of appreciation to the businessman for his contribution to the ministry and its food stamp fund.)

Only one who was there could know all the dynamics of making the decision to go to the Air Force Base. But these things are clear. There were certainly black leaders from the plantations capable of thinking of and carrying the plan through; and no one was forced to go—the fact that less than one-tenth of the total group participated would indicate considerable freedom of choice.

The Right Rev. Paul Moore, Jr., Suffragan Bishop of the Episcopal Diocese of Washington and chairman of the Commission on the Delta Ministry, during an informal press conference on February 7, said: "Wherever the idea might have come from, it was adopted with great enthusiasm." He also, without condoning the action, said the important point to consider was the deep sense of frustration that led to such a desperate act.[6]

Mrs. Lawrence, in her own inimitable fashion, summed it up: "You know, we ain't dumb, even if we are poor. We need jobs. We need food. We need houses. But even with the poverty program we ain't got nothing but needs. That's why we was pulled off that building that wasn't being used for anything. *The thing about property upset them, but the thing about poor people don't.* So there's no way out but to begin your own beginning, whatever way you can. So far as I'm concerned, that's all I got to say about the past. We're beginning a new future."[7]

Isaac Foster protests the ouster of the *poor peoples* from the Greenville Air Force Base February 1, 1966. Owen Brooks, Delta Ministry
staff, has his back to the camera.

MARY VARELA

Strike City, near Tribbett, Mississippi, during the bitterly cold days of January, 1966.

BRUCE HILTON

Exodus

We is like the children of Israel marchin' through the desert for the Promised Land. If we makes it, it'd be a miracle. I don't know which way this here thing is goin' to turn out, but I'm stickin' with the people. Me and my family's got no other place to go.

Mrs. Ida Mae Lawrence

The *poor peoples* had their answer from their government; they were ejected. So they began walking away, slipping and sliding in the mud-thaw on the side of the highway. After thirty hours of federal sanctuary, they now trudged the five miles back to town.

But something had happened in the tragic saga of the past few days. A sense of commonality had developed which would be the core for a wandering community; in their search for a life worth living, they would stumble, falter, and fragment for a period of more than two years. But their journey, their faith, would be a symbol of hope for many others rejected and dispossessed. They were, without laboring the image, embarking on their own exodus, to a "more promising land."

The immediate question was where to go. Even those who still had claim to tenant shacks would lose them after this event.

At least one place offered temporary refuge. During the occupation of the base, the poor people of Strike City, living out this winter in their battered tents—themselves having been evicted the previous May when they had asked "the man" for better wages—had sent part of their own meager food supplies to help feed the squatters. And they did more; they offered their five acres as a temporary haven for the displaced *peoples*.

Thus the new community center at Strike City, built over Christmas vacation by students from the University of Pennsylvania, became the second stop on this pathetic modern-day flight of faith. The very next day other families began to join them. A frail hope had been stirred and desperate men reached for it.

One writer described the mood on February 10:

"These people are down here to help folks like me. I ain't
got nothin' at all to lose by joinin'." His sentiments have been
echoed repeatedly, if cautiously, by farm Negroes throughout
the Delta since an abortive attempt was made last week to take
over an Air Force building at deactivated Greenville Air Force
Base to dramatize the plight of needy people.

The Delta Ministry pledge of support was obviously received loud and clear in frame houses along dirt roads of the
Mississippi countryside.

The Negro said he was one of scores being told by farmers
that they will not be needed in 1966 as laborers . . .[8]

In spite of the generosity of those at Strike City, things did not
go easy. Too many people swamped the few facilities; there was
almost no way to prepare, as an example, whatever food that could
be scrounged. The *poor peoples*, disorganized and bewildered by the
rapid developments of the past few days, soon recognized that it
had to move on.

To continue in uncertainty was not easily accepted by everyone,
upset several, and angered others. But Mr. Foster reflects: "I agreed
that there were too many of us to exist with the Strike City folks;
they only had five acres and there was not a chance of expanding."

Mud City

Their next stop was in Issaquena County, about forty-five miles south of Strike City in Tribbett. There they perched on a rather large, if unattractive, piece of land which they hoped to purchase from a Negro farmer; their only shelter was a huge circus-type tent which the Delta Ministry managed to locate and provide.

The stay itself was torture. The weather remained terrible; while not quite as cold, it rained constantly. Anyone venturing outside the tent sank into a mud bog. One man reckoned: "The mud's so deep pigs wouldn't mess with it."

Pressure from angry whites prevented the purchase of the land. They had to keep guards at night so that ominous threats of violence from white hoodlums would not catch them unprepared. Of the approximately seventy people who had made it this far, about half were ill, victims of the sharp winds and icy rains. Isaac Foster, moreover, noted one development which would become ever more crucial in the long days that lay ahead. "They just didn't seem to have the kind of motivation for the most part that the people at Strike City had. Their imagination, their knowledge, was much less; they couldn't accept the same responsibility."

The marvel is that the PPC survived this experience in what has been remembered as "Mud City." And with the thought of buying the land with money raised by friends and building more permanent shelters squelched, the *poor peoples* had to do something. After a week of misery, the Delta Ministry, ever involved and concerned, offered them once more the use of Mt. Beulah's campus until a way was found to secure land for them to build their own community.

Art Thomas, first director of the Delta Ministry, at Mt. Beulah, Mississippi. The old plantation house is in the background.

KEN THOMPSON

Mr. Beecham, a Delta Ministry employee, observes the charred remains of an eight-foot cross burned against the entrance sign at Mt. Beulah the night before Good Friday, 1967. Four Klansmen were seen placing the cross into place and setting it afire.

NASH BASOM

Mt. Beulah

MY PHYLOISPY OF LIFE
(A Rainsin the son)

I've offden, wounder and quostion myself about life.
Why dose man behave the way he dos? What is man
prpose? Will he ever achived his prpose? Then I ask
myself this, what is my prpose? Will I achived my
prpose?

Then say my prpose is my clibm 2 mountain, after
I've riched its highest peek what then. Does life end
there. Then if life is to countenure then where shell I
go. What will I seek?

Then out of my seeking what shell I find? What is
life, is it just a "dream that drys like a raisin in the son"
are is it like an actor who never been on stage, but leave
when lights are gone.

So I leave my quostion unanswer because I see myself without a future. For I am not a man, and I am a
man.

And until I am twice a man, I'll seek my propose.

And in the movie everybody had a dream, wonderful
dreams, that "dried like a Rainsin in the Son."

(The words above were written in 1965 by a young man who
had just seen *Raisin in the Sun* at Mt. Beulah; he had just come
to work with the Freedom Corps at that time. Now he is an important young member of the Delta Ministry staff.)

So they got together what was left and moved away from Mud
City, sadly mocking the hopes expressed by the DM only the week
before that "they will have moved hopefully for the last time."

That Mt. Beulah, located halfway between Jackson and Vicks-
burg right outside the tiny town of Edwards, was the next spot for
the nomads to pause, was not without irony.

An imposing old white plantation house dominates the highest
spot on the campus; this served, the story goes, as a slave market
in the 1830's. Later it became a junior college for Negroes conducted by the Disciples of Christ; its reputation at best was "Uncle

Tom-ish." For about a decade there had been no school and only occasional use of the campus. But the bursting out of civil rights activism had changed its image forever; Mt. Beulah, leased in 1965 by the Delta Ministry as the one place in the state where integrated conferences could be held in relative safety, had housed the office of the controversial Child Development Group of Mississippi (CDGM) in 1965, and hosted other projects by SNCC, CORE, FDP, and community (local) development groups. Now Mt. Beulah was under constant attack by Mississippi "red necks" as well as more genteel racists like Sen. John Stennis. The senator succeeded in forcing CDGM to leave Mt. Beulah for Jackson before it got refunded in its second (1966) year. (An unsubstantiated story circulates which provides its own kind of irony; a top official of the tiny Edwards bank secretly pleaded long and hard with Sen. Stennis to leave CDGM at Beulah. The once-hostile community had prospered and the bank had handled approximately $1,500,000 for CDGM alone. In short, they'd like both to be hostile and prosperous.)

The nine buildings (including three large dormitories; two smaller ones; a mess hall; administration, classroom, and library center; reception and office center, and a utility shed) offered a welcome refuge. It was a time to pause, to take stock, to heal the psychological and physical wounds of the past few hectic weeks, to begin to think through the organizational forms of the PPC, and to look to the day when they would be on their own *land*. Other families began to turn up and at one time, almost two hundred men, women, and children had found their way to the relative security of Mt. Beulah. Without doubt all-out recruiting and publicity would have increased their numbers a hundredfold. The *Memphis Commercial-Appeal* had written: "Delta farmers now seem acutely aware that the controversial National Council of Churches' unit has pipelines flowing freely into their previously impenetrable lands, and has successfully translated its message of help in securing jobs, food, housing, income and job training."[9]

Those involved in the ministry would have said it another way, talking of the incredible needs and what the slightest spark of hope could create; but the sentiment was obviously correct. The facts were, of course, that by standing beside the poor they had completely taxed the resources of the shakily financed DM. It reluctantly had to slow down the influx of refugees. (As it was, the budget was far overspent on the PPC and precipitated a severe crisis for the DM later that year.)

But the faith of the PPC was rewarded. On April 8, 1966, "The Poor Peoples Students Speak," a teen-age news sheet, reported:

". . . the land was finally bought yesterday. When the adults heard about it in their class, they let out a cheer . . . It has three houses, three trucks, five tractors, one combine and one store. There are also other farm tools available. It has twenty acres of wheat already planted.

"The poor peoples are still asking other poor to join us in building this new city."

A 400-acre farm near Greenville had been purchased after long negotiation with a reluctant white family. They would not have sold it to the PPC if they had not been leaving the state the day after the transaction. An anonymous northern friend had advanced a $70,000 loan to allow the PPC to make a down payment.

After hours of discussion about which crop to plant, they decided to go with soybeans. This, they determined, was best for them. They were in unanimous agreement with one man who said, "Gonna do anythin' but chop cotton again."

(George Scott, star first baseman of the Boston Red Sox baseball team, comes from Greenville; he said once in a TV interview that one reason he was a good baseball player was to assure that he never again would have to chop cotton.)

During May, the *land* was planted; housing was not available and during the work, the men piled into a variety of vehicles early each morning for the two-hour trip to *their* fields. Only those chosen to guard the *land* overnight remained there.

Classes, with tireless volunteers and staff manning the chalk, were conducted each morning for the children, women, and others not on the *land*. Some attempted literacy training, with particular emphasis on reading a ballot; there were sessions on Negro history, the rights and responsibilities of citizenship, and the theoretical bases of cooperative businesses. Not that anyone would recognize such formal nomenclature for the casual combination of group dynamics, gripe session, practical discussion ("Look—one more time—if everybody throws a coke bottle on the ground, we all gonna break our necks") mixed with some ingenious teaching of a more factual nature.

Sewing classes were conducted for the women and they both repaired their own tattered garments and began to produce some new clothes. What would become the Freedomcrafts workshops later on originated during this time as men got training using more sophisticated tools than many of them had seen.

Several have remarked that toilet training for those who had never known about more than outdoor johnnies at best was about as difficult as any part of their life together. Some were physically frightened of the flushing toilet; children, conversely, were fascinated with it and flushed it constantly. But young and old alike were known to have bowel movements alongside the toilet, not in it. And on at least one occasion, a man proudly used the newfangled gadget and then reverted to his old custom of covering his trail by piling stones into the bowl.

Three evenings a week the Poor Peoples Conference met in a long, often stormy, town meeting, arguing, clarifying, questioning; in short, taking the first steps toward the move to the *land*. It was primer work in the democratic process for people, most of whom couldn't read the phrase, certainly couldn't define it, but in a rudimentary way were beginning to practice it, many for the first time ever.

Two illustrations may help point to the possibility and the problem of the developing community.

In June, 1966, I received permission from the teacher and several members to attend an adult literacy class. As I, the only white in the room, took my seat, a middle-aged Negro, eyes downcast, apology all over his face—a shuffling caricature of a man—said to me, a total stranger: "Would you 'scuse me, mister? I'm just gonna get something to smoke. Be right back to class, I sure will."

Within the hour, an older, illiterate woman stopped the class proceedings, looked straight across the room at me, and demanded: "Can somebody tell me what this strange white man doin' here?"

My halting response that I was there as a friend seemed to satisfy and the class-cum-town meeting proceeded, meandering through a complex of elementary teaching points—how to make change, answer the telephone, read electric light meters; it also involved community decisions—who was to work where, how to improve sanitary conditions, and ways for better laundry collection.

One leaves such an experience with a completely ambiguous emotion. While marveling at the newfound individuality of the woman who apparently would not speak in public about anything when she had arrived, a human being so conditioned by his relation to "the man" that he has to seek the approval of a white intruder to retrieve forgotten cigarettes overwhelms. In such lie the problem and the promise of Freedom City, then and now.

Isaac Foster expressed it: "With a few exceptions, we were dealing with the discarded ruins of the plantations; it was really tough to rebuild enough spirit to get them to accept any responsibility. But that's really what we were trying to do during those days at Mt. Beulah."

Violence always hung over Mt. Beulah as an external threat; shots were fired into the camp several times, and a few crosses were burned. It was also a constant internal problem. Individuals had quarrels that brought bloodshed but not death. More serious were the habits of a small group of out-of-staters who had come in during the earlier civil rights days; they had no roots and wandered from hot spot to hot spot, picking up the name "boppers" along the way. It was no secret that many had serious psychological hang-ups; one psychiatrist said several were obviously psychotic. This presented the DM with a difficult dilemma. It did not want to alienate them completely, yet it had to be far enough removed so that the Ministry would not be destroyed by a possible destructive act.

Their presence at Beulah was constantly divisive. It all came to a public head when two or three of the boppers went to New York City and staged a sit-in at the National Council of Churches. They accused the Delta Ministry of ousting them and of exploiting the poor people of Mississippi. Officials acted swiftly to bring the officers of the PPC to confront the demonstrators and deny their charges; these representatives of the people defused the situation and, shortly afterward, the malcontents returned to Mt. Beulah. They were asked to leave by the PPC, but when they left, they took with them several tents—something of a pay-off—and a couple families.

The difficulty of letting people grow by making their own decisions while still feeling responsible to help protect them from exploitation is illustrated in this incident.

It was not easy, obviously. Just one more example: if some of the *boppers* were firing pistols at buildings and threatening to kill staff members, what did one do when there were no police to call? Fortunately for the *poor peoples* on both counts, the strength of several persons in the group, quite often women, rose up at the crucial points. Several of the young vital members of a group called Freedom Corps, led by Isaac Foster, finally saw to it, with a show of physical force, that the *boppers* did leave.

June brought its own sudden infusion of drama; James Meredith was shot down outside Hernando, Mississippi, and suddenly the eyes of the nation were on the state again. It was election time and the DM was not enthusiastic about yet another "demonstration"; to most, time was awfully precious to sacrifice on something that did not offer long-range possibilities. But there was little choice and Mr. Owen Brooks, now acting director of the Delta Ministry, marched almost the whole way. He was instrumental in working with a core group of Mississippi leaders to demand that the march change its focus to voter registration, which meant selecting a less direct route. Other staff members helped find supplies, provide communications, and maintain liaison. Most of the *poor peoples* were in Jackson for the culminating day of that march.

But as June became July, the group became more and more restless. "When do we go to the *land*?" They were held up by the difficulty in securing temporary housing.

In the meantime, one word filled the air constantly, the sustaining idea, the grace note in a life that needed at least one hint of certainty. *The land! The land!* The word permeated the group consciousness, assuming mystic, almost cultic dimensions. They had joined together out of desperation; they were sustained through the long dreary months of upheaval, discomfort, and uncertainty by the hope of making it to the *land*. Although I never heard it sung there, surely Woody Guthrie's "This Land Is Our Land" was the subconscious music that accompanied the journey.[10]

The mood of the Delta Ministry supported this dream; the staff had come to feel increasingly that more emphasis needed to be placed on long-range education and economic development programs and institutions that the Negro community could control; this was something of a shift from the earlier civil rights stage (the feeling that it made no difference if one had the civil right of eating in a public restaurant if he didn't have the money to buy a meal). They, and the *poor peoples*, were not the only ones talking about possible styles for a "new community." Others were also searching for ways the black man might develop for himself his forms of political, social, and economic action.

One illustration comes from an article in the *New South*, entitled: "Proposed: A Kibbutz in Mississippi."

> The Mississippi Negro, especially in rural areas, has been forced to live for generations in social, economic, and political dependence on the southern white. . . . Due to the constricting control of the white community, few cracks have opened spontaneously in the existing social and economic power structure that would provide the opportunity for this constructive institution-building. In this situation, any chance to develop responsible group action with sensitive outside consultants represents an extremely valuable experience as a learning process for the local participants and the organizers, and if successful, its ramifications as a model for action could be widespread.[11]

Two citizens of Freedom City with the prefabricated plastic *plydom* houses in the background. These were the first homes for the *peoples* at Freedom City.

KEN THOMPSON

The debris after heavy winds and rains ripped the *plydom* houses to shreds November 10, 1966.

KEN THOMPSON

Freedom City

Poor people supposed to be
    lazy
That's what the rich folks
    say
But what I want to know
    is
Did you ever see what kind of
    work
Poor folks got to
    do
Just to stay
    poor?
          (By a citizen of Freedom City)

The *poor peoples* pulled together their few belongings and made their last trek; this would really be their final move. They were going to their *land*, awaited for hundreds of years; they were going home.

But *homes* were still a long way off. A Florida manufacturer had supplied twenty-five plastic, prefabricated *plydom* houses for $500 each. These were to be the temporary dwellings of the *peoples*. The farm buildings already there were turned into an office, dispensary, and cafeteria.

Mr. Isaac Foster, director of the PPC during the move to the *land*, said:

"The problems when we moved were overwhelming. Some of the people had done carpentry work all of their lives and had worked on a plantation or on a farm but when they got to the *land* it was a psychological reason why they couldn't work. The men who had been carpenters, suddenly they couldn't read a square, they couldn't use a saw, a hammer, anymore. And it was because they had never done anything for themselves, they thought they had to have someone to tell them what to do; in that sense they had never done anything for themselves, but always for the 'boss man.' They were looking for a substitute for him. But finally we began to pass that stage.

"We had meetings every night to talk about what we were going to do the next day. We divided up the work hours, assigned different jobs, and, you know, talked about roles; but that didn't work because, gee, they just couldn't accept the initiative to do something.

"We even tried my becoming the boss man one week and everything worked better on the surface but we decided that it's better my not becoming that, so we got rid of the idea. You know, if they didn't want to do it for themselves, sooner or later, they would go into a slowdown, where they only looked like they were working, like they did on their boss man on the plantation. No substitute for learning to do it because they wanted to do it.

"But you know what helped most? The people from Strike City came; they wouldn't wait around for someone else, but they would say, 'Come on, let's get to work!' And then they would start doing things. This was the thing I noticed that influenced, motivated the people at Freedom City most, to do any kind of work. Strike City was a big aid. Which pleased me very much."

One man refused to work on his own, complaining because everything had not been made ready for him. Mr. Foster talked to him, gently but firmly, "You've been with us all these months now and, hell, you don't understand yet. Ain't nobody gonna make this ready for you 'cause you ain't working for 'the man' now. You working for yourself. For yourself, you the man! You understand?"

Sadly, this particular person probably never will. For every one of these people in the original group—so broken, twisted, deprived, used up—who does, two surely cannot. A *New York Times* reporter observed the Freedom City experiment during this time and called it a "desperate experiment." Unlike many past efforts at a new community, he felt, this one was based on desperation rather than idealism or intellectual curiosity.[12]

By fits and starts, the *peoples* adjusted to life on the *land*. Bedlam prevailed in their dining hall, a converted store of the type often seen on drives through the South with Tube Rose signs and a Coca-Cola thermometer on the side; but they had food, inadequate though it was. Their shower was in a converted silo; it was picturesque only so long as one did not have to shower there himself. The *plydom* houses were close together and the families piled on top of each other, but they were livable and the folks at Freedom City hardly knew that in some worlds separate rooms exist. Water and sanitary facilities were extremely limited and came close to being a serious health hazard. (Health officials from Greenville criticized the conditions severely; one of the staff members responded: "It's bad but then it did give the families a new experience; they had never in their lives seen a health official, now one suddenly got awfully interested in them.") While the money has now been found for wells and a sewage system, even in mid-1968 the water and sanitary conditions would appall most outsiders—like the conditions which prevail on most of the plantations.

The old machinery balked and stalled; the first bean crop, planted late, improperly cultivated, harvested without directions from an experienced "man," hardly paid for the seed, fertilizer, and mechanical costs. Certainly it did not begin to return the $16,000 needed the following April 7, to meet the first mortgage payment and interest on the bank note.

School time came up and the children from Freedom City integrated Riverside High in Avon, a few miles away. Regular school for almost any of them would have been a painful adjustment; here they had to fight for their very lives physically each day. Some teachers mistreated them, gangs of white kids chased and often attacked them. The principal was at best sullen. Running that gauntlet to return to the sanctuary of their *plydom* huts was not the end of the day by any means. Every night staff members and sympathetic friends from nearby put them through a tutoring program from 7-9 P.M., attempting to interpret—by guesswork often —what had been taught and anticipate what should be looked to for the next day.

When Foster left in September to enroll in college in New York City, he was replaced as director of the PPC by Mr. John Bradford. Bradford was a native of Mound Bayou, the all-Negro town near Cleveland, Mississippi, founded by a slave of Jefferson Davis in the 1870's. He had been out of the state to college in Michigan for a couple of years and was working in Greenville when asked to come to Freedom City. (He remained at the job through the summer of

1967.) While discussing the problem of developing a routine of attending school for these children, he commented: "It took a full-scale organizational effort to wake people up and to make sure they got off to school at all. If you miss thirty days you get kicked out of school for the rest of the year, and most of them weren't very far from that by Christmas. We had one lady who was particularly bad about not getting up and seeing that her kids went to school. The group, at the suggestion of Curtis [Hoskins, the nineteen-year-old president of the PPC] and me, made her the chairman of the committee to get them to school. She had my clock and it meant that she had to get up first, get her kids up, then get all the others up."

Some semblance of regularity began to work its way into the life of the new community. And they continued to meet often, growing in the ability to think about what they wanted and how to tell it to others.

Then, with terrible suddenness, disaster struck. During the night of November 10, a fierce storm blew across the flat Delta and high winds, approaching tornado intensity, ripped the plastic shells to shreds. As the only home his family had ever really controlled was swept up into the wind, one youngster said it looked like a "kite over the Delta." A few were left standing but all were beyond repair. Inexplicably, the only injury came to one child on whom a dresser had toppled during the storm.

The houses had been guaranteed to last five years; but, as the Bible reminds us, the poor get poorer. They never collected on the loss.

Nor did they receive help from anyone white in Mississippi other than the Methodist leadership. A foundation approached the Red Cross but should have known that it could not help during a holiday weekend (Veteran's Day). Civil Defense offered bedding and lumber; then Civil Defense retracted the offer. Miss Evelyn Gandy, the same state welfare director, talked to the Civil Defense Official. That was enough to kill the offer.

But emergency funds did come in from several national denominational offices and truckloads of food, clothing, and bedding were sent from others. The barn and scattered tenant shacks which came with the *land* were hastily made endurable, if not really livable.

Sitting in the comfort of a New York apartment, watching with shock as the evening news suddenly zoomed in on the face of Curtis Hoskins standing beside the shambles of his hut, the extremely pessimistic words of a not unsympathetic member of the white community in Greenville two months earlier suddenly came back:

"Freedom City has all the conditions of disaster about it. It's pitiful; and if there's a fire or an epidemic, the Delta Ministry will be ruined. That land is awful and they can't ever make it pay; and those people can't ever exist without complete dependency on somebody."

I hadn't agreed at the time, but it was hard now to ignore those words. That winter was certainly the nadir of the life on the *land*. The morale of the *peoples* was low and at times some of them came dangerously close to thinking that they didn't have to keep on struggling, that someone would look after them, however poorly. Hopeful signs—the developing determination of those children who could learn to stay in school, the planting of a winter wheat crop, increased efficiency with Freedomcrafts—were more than offset by the deepening crisis. There still wasn't enough to do to keep people really busy, and that bred trouble. Some families left, partly out of discouragement; one family, threatened by loss of their meager social security checks if they did not leave, had to move and left a major gap at Freedom City. Some of the staff and friendly observers were deeply discouraged. A great deal had been put into Freedom City at the expense of other work, and the model of hope that seemed so important was turning into the project that promised now to pull the whole ministry down as it sank.

Personal tensions among the residents increased. They became focused around one man who was mistreating his wife while at the same time openly spending nights with a young single woman on the *land*.

Mr. Hoskins recalled: "This kept on and on, making trouble and we cannot make progress with somebody pulling us down like that. And we told him, if he didn't do better, he'd have to go. . . . We've got a way with troublemakers and so the *poor peoples* called a meeting and laid the facts on the line like they were. He had to go, he was pulling us another way. We know men's going to be men, but the disturbance was too much. He left and went to Shaw, but he's in jail now. The other woman went with him.

"That's the only one we had to ask to leave since Mt. Beulah. And things seemed to get a lot better after that."

Which was true. No one seems to know quite why. There were probably a number of reasons. Acting as a group to ask the man to leave whom many of them feared provided group catharsis. (Even Mr. Bradford, an impressively strong man of about 6' 2" said: "Charlie was a booger, ohhhh he was rough. He would tear up stuff for no reason anybody could see.") The group was maturing in spite of the difficulties. They had made extensive plans for the new bean crop and were able to repair the machines they had for a total cost of $1800; it had been feared at first that they would have to purchase a new tractor and combine. And perhaps it was because spring was in the air.

Whatever it was, some breaks began to go their way. Housing had improved with the purchase of an old Elk's Club; this was moved to the *land* and divided into three units with two apartments each. Freedom City was told, in what was obviously a decision custom-made to harass the community, that it could not receive food stamps for use in its community kitchen. This meant that the *peoples* had to use what little money they had accumulated in their treasury to buy used stoves and refrigerators so individuals could do their own cooking. But what seemed at first unfortunate turned out to be an important new direction. Almost immediately, the same people who complained so bitterly about having to buy the appliances were proud of them. Life as a family unit began to take on more meaning as they at least had privacy from others, if not from each other.

No one had known where the $16,000 mortgage payment would come from. But on February 26, the "Wild Goose Committee," a Dutch organization which makes a five-minute appeal over IKOR radio each Sunday for contributions to a different project around the world, made Freedom City the special emphasis. Earlier IKOR-TV network had shown an hour-long special on Freedom City (something never done by U.S. television) and the Delta Ministry on Christmas Day, repeating it on February 5. When the mail with gifts began pouring in, the "Wild Goose Committee" had collected a total of 40,000 guilders (approximately $11,000), treble that usually donated. On April 4 the treasurer of Freedom City received a draft for that amount and on April 7, the payment was met.

Fertilizer and feed money, which had looked doubtful during the hard winter, was raised out of $2800 cleared on the late wheat crop, plus a private contribution. By May 1, all the men, women, and children, when not in school, were at work, seeding well-prepared and fertilized fields. Soybeans, wheat, and vegetables were all planted.

OEO had granted $199,805 to the Delta Opportunities Corporation for administrative and training costs for a project in self-help housing, but it awaited a matching grant from another foundation toward a water and sewage system and materials for the actual buildings. (The DOC is a non-profit organization, with a biracial, all-Mississippi board, set up by the DM in 1965 as an independent, non-profit conduit for developmental programs. It relates to nine counties in Mississippi and has taken over most of the administration for Freedom City.) By September, 1967, the Ford Foundation had granted $160,000 to match the OEO funds.

Gradually, the corner was turned; while the money would not solve all the needs of Freedom City by any means (the original request to OEO had included both a medical program and job training for women heads-of-household, not eligible for training under the present grant), the *land* now gave real signs of being a viable new city.

There would be job training in carpentry, plumbing, brick masonry, and electrical wiring. The trainees would build their own homes and many should be able to find jobs as helpers within the Greenville area. Most important, the project would mean that about thirty-five families would be added to Freedom City with male heads-of-household. Many of these would have more skills and individuality to bring to a truly living community. Further, twenty-five more families were included in the training program than in the housing grant; additional funds were being sought to allow them too to live on the *land*. It is conceivable that by the summer of 1969, seventy-five families and more than 500 people will be living at Freedom City.

United Church Women provided a licensed practical nurse to offer health education and nutrition training for the women. Another foundation has given funds for complete physical examinations and dental checks for about 150 persons.

Mrs. Ora Wilson, recording secretary of Freedom City, and her helper began to make some money personally and to provide much less expensive but, nevertheless, new—indeed tailored—clothes to residents of Freedom City and the surrounding area in the spring of 1967.

The most colorful project among the women was the redecoration of one of the houses, under careful supervision, to teach them by doing how to decide on furnishings, color combinations, and paints. It now serves as a demonstration house.

Two white families were in the group in the spring of 1968 and others have shown interest in coming to Freedom City. Last summer there was hard work on a baseball diamond and one of the twenty-acre plots is being developed as a park for the whole community.

Also during the spring of 1967 many of the men at Freedom City got into training programs in Greenville. For some the vocational training, and the basic education courses which accompany it, will not take. One man in his early thirties, broken beyond repair, will almost surely never be able to hold a job. (He said that " 'rith'tic" was hardest for him; sometimes he lay awake at night worrying about 2 x 5. "Sometimes hit comes out to be one more'n you think, sometimes one less.") But the stipend he received while in the training program was almost the first money he had ever handled, and it did wonders for his self-confidence. If the kind of community complex develops that is envisioned, a certain number like him can still find ways to stay independent by being custodians, watchmen, stock men in a store, or—while they will not use the crops forever as a major source of income, they will continue to grow crops—to work in the fields. Similarly, two women heads-of-household opened a store with a small stock in late 1967, and they should be ready to run a complete business when the houses are finished.

The tantalyzing promise of a small factory to be located in the neighborhood was often dangled in front of Freedom City; but national corporations who discussed this possibility always argued that they had to wait for evidence of a "going" town. It was a vicious circle, for a business would have insured such a town; but there is increasing evidence that the people will be there, capable of working in such a factory. If one is secured, the economic future of Freedom City would look just that much brighter.

Mrs. Thelma Barnes, primary person from the DOC and the DM now responsible for Freedom City, says: "We hope that this will mean the development of an entire area, not just a place called Freedom City. We could have a shopping center kind of thing there, with barber shop, laundromat, restaurant, dress shop. And I have in my dreams that the people in Freedom City will want to do some kinds of things eventually which aren't really done for Negroes in Mississippi at all. We need homes for the elderly. We need a children's home; there is no foster home at all and if something happens, you just depend on families to keep kids. That means a lot of six-year-olds looking after a whole raft of younger kids. We need neighborhood nurseries and a day-care center.

"And we want a school nearby and before long we should be able to build a church."

During the first months of 1968, the training program was in full swing in Greenville, under the direction of Mr. McKinley Martin, a Negro with a master's degree, hired by DOC to develop this project and help the DOC begin to spread out. Trainees not only build small-scale wood or concrete block houses over and over again, perfecting their skills, but also produce tables, chairs, and other items immediately usable in the DOC offices, at Freedom City and in their own homes.

By January 1, 1969, six houses were practically completed and the foundations for several others had been finished. Each will have an acre of land where chickens, gardens, and flowers will be in vogue.

There is evidence, at the beginning of 1969, that the DOC will indeed be able to find funds for projects affecting areas much larger than Feedom City. More than $300,000 from various government agencies and private foundations was going to be made available for more self-help housing, day-care nursing, canning projects, and for emergency food and medical relief in a five-county area.

In the late summer of 1966, I wrote:

"The stakes are large—for the PPC, for the Delta Ministry, for the Church, for the Delta Negro, for us all. A great deal has been gambled on this model. If it fails, the Delta Ministry may fail, and the presence of the Church with the dispossessed in Mississippi may be cut off for years to come. If it succeeds, there may well be the potential for multiple developments that will not only offer hope to some tens of thousands of Delta Negroes, who now must choose between the frying pan of present Mississippi life and the fire of the big-city ghetto, but also offer redemption to Mississippi's closed and diseased society.

"Ida Mae Lawrence, secretary and one of the most determined, articulate members of the PPC, stated: 'People all over the Delta are watching us. If we do succeed . . . they'll come by the hundreds to get in it with us.'

"Many people are critical of Freedom City, but most of the criticism missed the point. Sure, it seems a frail plant, surrounded by a hostile society, limited by its own ability to grow. I don't know how it will make it. But the cost of its failure is unthinkable."[13]

The frail plant has, against imponderable odds, taken root and gives encouraging signs of growth. The *peoples*, in this modern-day exodus, have had their dream of what life on the *land* could be to sustain them when they were lost, as their "pillar of cloud by day and the pillar of fire by night" (Exod. 13:22).

"Now faith is the substance of things hoped for, the evidence of things not seen . . ." (Heb. 11:1, K.J.V.).

Mrs. Fannie Lou Hamer, Mississippi Freedom Democratic Party delegate to the 1964 Atlantic City Democratic Party primary, who has said, "I'm sick and tired of being sick and tired."

KEN THOMPSON

Four young residents of Freedom City, Mississippi.

TOGE FUJIHIRA

THE FACES OF
FREEDOM CITY

FREEDOM CITY IS PEOPLE; the Delta Ministry is people. However gripping or important the collective experience of a group, the danger in writing about it is that individuals as people are overlooked. Human beings have been involved in Freedom City and they still have their own needs and fears, their own contributions and liabilities.

It is as persons meeting, talking to one another across vast differences, that the inhabitants of Freedom City come to me, first and last.

Each has his own story and any description of the difficult journey to Freedom City ought to offer a few brief word portraits. These will include a young resident, an older woman, a white newcomer, a staff member, and, in a longer piece, one who has left Mississippi to return after further training.

The words are their words, transmitted as faithfully as possible from taped interviews. Only the order has been edited, to give a sense of cohesiveness to statements that grew out of much longer, and often quite casual, conversations.

Curtis Hoskins, president of the Poor Peoples Conference, and his family.

NASH BASOM

The President of
the Poor Peoples
Conference

Mr. Curtis Hoskins was elected president of the PPC in 1967 when he was only nineteen. That one so young had been selected for this responsibility highlights a continuing problem of Freedom City and, more tragically, of all Mississippi. Not surprisingly, those above twenty-five who can break through the bonds of habit and perceive a new kind of life are almost always the women. A civil rights truism has it that if a man has not taken his stand by his early twenties, he will have surrendered too much ever to recover. If he escaped emotional and physical deformity at birth and during early childhood, he often has left the state altogether. As Freedom City knows from experience, a true community cannot be developed around stronger older women and the very young.

"Being president, 'specially me being so young, is lots of responsibility. But John Bradford [then DM staff member responsible to Freedom City], any time I picks up the phone and say, 'John, come out here, I need help,' he tells me things or comes on out from Greenville. You know, the *peoples* here have a little misunderstanding or somethin'. I talk with 'em but sometimes I don't do any good and he come around and talk to 'em and they get cool. We've become somethin' of a great big family; I may raise cain with my neighbor but still, anything happen, I am ready to die for him.

"I feel right now likes we is makin' progress at Freedom City. We movin' and the thing I hope is for the people here to think what they want, to try to get ideas. I think things, Bradford thinks things, but I want them to bring ideas up. It might be better'n ours and I want them to come up and tell us, face to face. We'll be glad to work with their plans and I want everybody to make up their own minds."

As we sat around a frail table in what served as the dining room and held two cot beds, the TV in the next room advertised Right Guard spray deodorant and "up, up and away" with TWA. A child of about eight went to the small but neat refrigerator and got out a popsicle Hoskins had brought back from Greenville with him that afternoon.

"When we first came here we ate all together in the dining hall. But the children was runnin' all over the place or throwing rice across the table. It's better now to have our own things to cook on. We have two white families here; they are just like I am, poor, no money, trying to do better. They seem to get along all right with Negroes; they were mistreated by the 'boss man,' just like us.

"Rest of the people feels the same way I do. We all pullin' for the same thing. You can't tear a crowd apart if you pullin' for the same thing; it's easy to pull one man apart. What white men there is around here don't like for their tenants to mess with us but they gettin' better. And we are gettin' to know peoples."

HOWELL: "Are you happy on the *land*?"

HOSKINS: "They's no foolin' that we've had a lot of hard times. But we are still happy on the *land*. Yeh, since we on the *land*, I went back to my hometown about two weeks ago and found out I didn't like it no more. I was on a plantation and I could never consider that my home; if I would, I'd be making a mistake because it belonged only to the white man. Here, it's a lot different because I can consider this as my home. I don't have to worry nothin' about the man sayin', 'if you don't pull your son out of school and chop my cotton, you gonna have to leave.'

"My hometown? Sunflower City! The plantation we was on the man was also the deputy. Peoples up in Drew would have a civil rights meetin' and him and his partner would go up there and shoot over the church and catch a few Negroes walking around outside and he'd beat 'em up. When the Movement first came to my hometown you wouldn't hardly see more'n one Negro wear a civil rights pin [white and black shaking hands] but I got aholt of one.

"First time I came home with it my mother asked me to take it off 'cause those who were wearin' them were gettin' beaten up and fired. This was in 1963. But then it changed so much and I'm glad. This work—civil rights work—is kind of dangerous but it's worth it; I enjoy it . . .

"When I was workin' on elections at Crystal Springs, representing Ed King who was runnin' for the MFDP office, I met up with a couple problems I wasn't able to cooperate with. They had teachers teaching the children—Negro teachers—that civil rights work was wrong. White peoples' always payin' preachers to say it was wrong. Negro principals would fire teachers who didn't say it was wrong also. Lots had been paid to talk bad about civil rights workers."

HOWELL: "How did you hear about Mt. Beulah?"

HOSKINS: "We left Sunflower in 1964, no 1966; the whole family. I wouldn't dare leave 'em. We left because we had been plannin' for some time to leave; the boss man had changed. My father was too old to work and even when we got out of school, there was no work. I begin to see that this man didn't care whether we are hungry or not. Only he's interested in his tractor drivers. I decided for us to go somewhere we could make progress.

"There's some men goin' around tellin' about Mt. Beulah and the *poor peoples* and we had heard about it anyway. We decided to go.

"You know, me'n my whole family started to Chicago once but only got as far as Memphis and my grandmother asked us to come back and we did. I never got that far again. And I'm glad we're here rather'n up there. 'Though Mississippi is a rotten state, I'm goin' to fight here where I know it rather than there.

"I've been married two years and I'm like this. The average Negro has a house full of children, but me, if my daughter wants somethin', I'd like to be able to get it for her. It takes a great deal of money to raise a large family well . . ."

HOWELL: "Some families have left Freedom City this year. Why?"

HOSKINS: "It's kind of hard to say why. Some gets discouraged. One man was goin' to lose his social security. It's been a hard time on the *land*. And we have this kind of problem here too. You can understand it when you have womens without husbands here. This one had her husband get messed up with a woman down the road and she sees all this and it cause a disturbance. This one cat was bad at that, but we could have stood it and all if he didn't come back and beat her up, all the time, anywhere.

"For me the best thing this year has been this weldin' trainin'. I go into Greenville and 8:30-12:30 is basic education. 1-5 is welding, the way to hold one's hands, different ways of doin' it. We gets an allowance and someday we'll have our homes here and if things go right, I'll have a welding job. It's a good thing."

The
Sewing
Lady

Lines cut deep into her gaunt face, cured by a lifetime of exposure to the brutal Delta sun, hands calloused and yet graceful, bones pushing through skin taut from poor food—all give Mrs. Ora D. Wilson, recording secretary of the PPC, the appearance of being far older than her fifty years.

It was difficult to follow her soft words, in part because rock-and-roll music blared through the thin partition separating the Wilson's apartment in the converted Elk's Club from the neighbors. She sat, with unexpected poise, in a faded print dress on a bed with an incredible sway toward the middle. One heavier than Mrs. Wilson surely would not have been able to maintain balance.

She and several of her children have been with the group the whole difficult journey. "I was liss'nin on the radio and they said it was for poor peoples and, Lord knows, we were poor. Ever'body was hungry at that time and we sure was. So we went to join them at the Air Force Base where they was waitin' for food. But I got there too late. There was no food and so then we had no place to go. I've been with the *peoples* ever since.

"I was choppin' and pickin' cotton at Indianola on day-haul labor where I lived and we'd catch trips to anybody's plantation. I got to work in the good times at first from the last two weeks in May through August when the beans came in. It was five days a week for three dollars a day. He gave me all fifteen dollars, he didn't hold back none.

"When my husband left in 1963 I fed me and my four children home on that. I been choppin' cotton all my days, since I was about nine years old."

HOWELL: "Would you ever chop cotton again?"

WILSON: "No sir, if I could do anythin' else I'd do it rather than chop cotton. I done killed myself almost. I never liked choppin' but I didn't mind pickin' so much. It all gets you in the hot sun."

HOWELL: "How many children did you have and where are the others now?"

WILSON: "I got eight head of children in all. Oldest one is in St. Louis workin' in some kind of clothin' factory; he likes it all right. He went to stay with my baby brother. The next boy, Sandy Wilson, went to the Army and came out in 1965 and went to St. Louis.

"I got a letter from my other boy last week; he's in California and he told me he still in the Air Force. He was in Germany, that's where he was. Irene and Kathleen live with me, and Charles Lee left two days ago to try the Job Corps in Michigan. I hope he made it; ain't heard from him yet. And Sammy and Booker T. are here now."

Charles Lee is an unusually promising young man whom I had met in 1966. He had been an important part of the development of the group and, with training, his future looks bright. He plans to return to Mississippi, and, for the sake of others, the staff hopes so.

Sammy and Booker T., about fourteen and twelve, obviously are extremely bright. They had been a key part of the difficult first year at the integrated school. Earlier in our conversation, Mrs. Wilson had said that the school children wanted to go back to the segregated school during the coming year. Thus she was quite surprised when she heard Sammy say:

SAMMY: "We want to go back to Avon; don't want to go to that other school."

MRS. WILSON: "Well, I don't understand that. Y'all's got to make up your minds soon. When did you decide that?"

SAMMY: "I don't know, we just did."

HOWELL: "I heard you had a hard time at the school."

SAMMY: "Ohhh, yeah, it wasn't too easy . . . don't know."

HOWELL: "Did it get easier as the year went on?"

SAMMY: "Toward the end it got better. My teacher was nice but some were awful mean."

HOWELL: "How was the principal?"

SAMMY: "He was kind of in-between."

HOWELL: "How did you first get into the movement?"

MRS. WILSON: "I got involved in the movement because of these children. I was choppin' cotton in the fields at that time and leavin' them at home. Sammy here came to me and said, 'There's some folks at the school over there and I've been with them. They havin' a meetin' and wants you to come over there.' I said: 'I'll go some time.'

"Everyday I'd go home and was tired and they'd say, 'Come on over to the school.'

"One day I sent 'em some ice water over, and . . . well, that's the way I got interested, with these children. They give them some shoes and pants and then this woman came to my house. I wished I'd heard about it earlier.

"My husband works at the chemical plant but he's got another woman and didn't help with the family, but he never did do much. Lots of men ain't very good with families."

Several people close to Freedom City said that Mrs. Wilson, in her quiet way, was extremely important to the group. She put her boys to bed at eight every night even at Mt. Beulah and in the tents, and made sure that they went to school. According to one, "She does more by example than any ten lectures by outsiders."

Her special contribution had been to make sewing an increasingly important factor in the life of the "city." All the girls came to school wearing dresses she and her helper had made, and she was earning a little money this way. Eventually, they should be able to branch out to the whole community, helping themselves and saving others money and the trip into town.

"Cloth was give to us and they made me director of the sewin'. We got enough money to buy our own stuff and some special things that let us do better sewin'. And the money we make, we takes it and puts it back into the pot; that would pay for what we need. Two of us work sewin', from 9-12 and 1-4 ever' day. My mother taught me to sew. The machines were a gift to the *peoples* from some folks in Greenville."

HOWELL: "How do you feel now about Freedom City?"

WILSON: "I'm happy here at Freedom City now and I'll be even happier when we gets our houses. I'm workin' and don't have so many expenses as before. And things are lots better now than when we first came. Tent City was hard and we was awful confused at Mt. Beulah. But I've never been sorry to be with the *peoples*; at home I didn't get but one meal a day and sometimes nothin' at all."

This was in August, 1967, as she sat straight and still on the misshaped bed, two grandchildren scurried underfoot; Booker T. and Sammy scuffled in and out of the room with other boys. The noise from next door never ceased. I'll remember the dignity of Mrs. Ora Wilson, the sewing lady who sat there so calmly in the tight clutter of the two tiny rooms, for a long time.

The
White
Resident

In a development that no one would have predicted even weeks earlier, the first white residents came to Freedom City in July, 1967. Mr. James Allen moved his wife, and five children living at home, to one of the old tenant's shacks on the *land*. Not long afterward, another white family moved to Freedom City also.

The new additions created considerable conversation. It was an obvious plus for external public relations; no longer could the community be dubbed an "Indian Reservation" or racist in reverse. Their decision brought faint glimmers of hope that the developing city might someday be a place of freedom for all people, regardless of, etc. It was a minor, if important, reminder that 65 percent of those in serious poverty conditions in the United States are white.

Some, both of the *peoples* and the DM staff, thought the move came too early. Could the hard-won independence of the residents stand up under the greater sophistication of the whites? Could the *peoples* and the whites really get along? Could the whites stand the kind of isolation they would suffer from almost all other whites, because, as one person said, "they'll be lower on the social scale even than civil rights workers"? How could they explain it to those many black families who wanted to come to the *land* now, before the slow-moving housing program got underway?

The PPC made the decision after long debate. A year later it seems to have worked out reasonably well. Obviously, the request from both families was made in desperation, but one would add that both white families had to have something more that set them apart from people as poor as they. After all, the most violent hatred of blacks almost always comes from those on the lowest economic scales.

When Mrs. Allen talks, it is not in the drawl of the Mississippi white or the more difficult to decipher "mumble" of many of those on the *land*. She reveals, rather, the marked twang of the Arkansas mountains of her mother tongue.

"I didn't think I'd like it here at first, but it's nice. We got eight boys and one girl in all, but only five of 'em is here. Jim works as a mechanic; he's not well but poor people's got to keep goin'. But Jim can do that pretty well, long's he don't hafta go into the fields.

"We was on the Andrews' plantation after the strikers got throw'd off, but we left after six months. We went to Leland but Jim got hurt bad and couldn't work; he was off for the last eight months. We tried ever'where to get a job; they wouldn't hire Jim because he was crippled and because they knowed he'd turn them in if they didn't pay wages right. We lived on this road off and on and had driven past here; Freedom City was our last chance. We needed someone to help us and they did. They say they are to help those who need it, white or colored."

Her two youngest boys, about twelve and ten, came bursting into the house followed by several of the children who lived there also. A chicken was ricocheting around the living room, shrieking so piercingly that part of the tape, recording the conversation, is ruined; in the midst of this confusion, a monstrous dog fight breaks out on the rickety porch. She demands harshly that the dogs stop, and then shoos the whole works back into the yard, chicken included.

"If the plantation owner would stop and think, if it wasn't for the poor a tillin' his soil and workin' for him he wouldn't have these homes and big cars and somethin' to eat settin' on the table. Most of 'em, it belongs to the credit corporation and they still look down on us who do the work."

HOWELL: "You said you worked on the Andrews' plantation. You do mean the one where the strike started? Can you tell me about it?"

ALLEN: "That's the one. I wouldn't hardly know how to explain a man like that, he's awful! Can't nobody get along with him. I don't think he's got but about three families left but they're a movin' in and out all the time, don'cha know? The other family that just come told me he was supposed to pay one dollar an hour but he never did. He held it out on Jim but never did turn it in. He'd go to work at six and get in at dusk, six days a week. Held back $2 a day, paid him $6 with $240 on Christmas payback. Sometimes Jim would go down at 6 A.M. and it'd be wet and so he'd get Jim to give him a hand here and there; about ten he'd tell Jim that it was too wet, there'd be no work today.

"He'd not allow any visitors and he'd say, 'Who's that visitin' there? What does he want? They got no business here. I don't want 'em around.'

"Even my own children, he told not to come there. He didn't want us to go past the main road; I told him when he got the papers showing he owned that road, I'd gladly stay off.

"If you got sick, he ain't goin' to take you. He even 'chewed us out' for pickin' up pecans on another man's place when we had permission.

"My boys will go to school at Riverside over at Avon, same place as the colored kids go.

"We're eatin' better now; at first we had to give $8 for $48 in food but now we have to give $2 for $48 on food stamps. The Delta Ministry helps us out, don'cha know? Course it's about to go broke. If Thelma Barnes wasn't such a talker, we'd be in bad trouble.

"But we're glad to be here. Jim and John Bradford gets along real well. I told 'em they are more like brothers than a white and a nigra. And it's real interestin'. We even have foreigners here; Sunday we had them from six different countries. One from India had on a robe and sandals."

As did someone else who believed in the poor. He would surely have given the *poor peoples* His blessing when they decided to let poor whites take one of the premium empty places on the *land*.

The late Senator Robert F. Kennedy during his visit to Mississippi to investigate hunger in the Delta in 1967. His host for a major portion of the visit was Mrs. Thelma Barnes, Delta Ministry staff, seen at the left in the picture.

DAN GURAVICH

The
Tireless
Lady

Mrs. Thelma Barnes received national attention in 1967 when Sen. Robert Kennedy and Sen. Joseph Clark, visiting Mississippi to verify reports of severe hunger, spent much of their time ignoring regular politicos and allowing themselves to be shown things "like they are" by Mrs. Barnes. She and the senators were on the front page of the *New York Times* the next day and she made all the TV reports.

Her involvement in the investigation was considerably more than ceremonial, however. For Mrs. Barnes has spent her life in service to the people of the Delta and she knows them and their problems. The astute senators had simply found the person most able to point them to what they needed to see.

Mrs. Barnes has placed her indefatigable energy into a complex number of tasks since coming to the staff of the Delta Ministry; her style, to the point but with a soft and compassionate edge, has done more than perhaps any other single factor to make the DM a more acceptable agency in the eyes of the whites in towns like Greenville. She has not compromised, but as a Negro native, she has been able to communicate to an unusually broad spectrum. And she is, increasingly, being heard.

In the summer of 1967, things were very tense among the black teen-agers of Greenville. Mrs. Barnes recalls: "The Southside group of young people invited me to a meeting. They aired out their grievances; they were all ready to cut loose with a riot at that point. After they had finished and they were all 'gung ho' to go, I started questioning them about their readiness.

"Then they said, 'We don't want any Tom's in here!'

"I said, 'I'm not against your moving, because it takes movement to get things accomplished. The movement you've done so far has made policemen come in here now in marked cars. And they've got Negro policemen in marked cars now, so you've really

done something. But have you presented your grievances to anyone?'

"They hadn't, so they began to list them and they decided that
there were a lot of things they hadn't thought of. So some of those
unemployed now have gotten jobs and we have a teen-center which
they run themselves. The mayor, chief of police, chamber of com-
merce, and a few interested businessmen have helped. But the city
as a whole is not ready to do anything meaningful, so it means that
someone who really wants to do anything has a difficult time doing
it. Greenville's good reputation, in some instances, is harmful to
progress because everyone thinks we've got it like it ought to be."

Mrs. Barnes' record testifies to itself. In order to find out more
about what combination of things produced such a unique individual, I asked her to tell something of her life story.

"I was born about thirty-five miles south of here in Grace,
Mississippi. My grandfather was a Baptist minister, and I grew up
in a religious environment. His library was extensive, with all kinds
of books in it, particularly religious and those designed for children.
I used to go into seclusion sometimes, either with paper dolls or
children's religious books.

"Because of this I was always pretty much top of my class,
winning spelling bees and things like that. My mother and grandmother and aunt were teachers. My aunt was interesting. Her father
was a white man, and he lived with her mother in that little community. Grace, actually, was quite a different community for that
time, but it's died down now. Before my day it was a real river town,
with bawdy houses and tough saloons, but when I came along it
was a nice place to grow up.

"My aunt taught because she loved it, not because she needed
the living. And the school was pretty good; it gave me a good
foundation in the first eight grades.

"I came from a family that thought everyone should read and
write; in the fourth grade I had to teach all the old people to write
their names, read simple sentences. I used to go around to various
houses and help people order from catalogues. I'd ride my bike
and then mail their orders and their letters. They called me,

'School teacher.' Anyway, I really had to serve the community.

"That's what I've always *had* to do. In coming up I had a real Christian experience; I mean I'm not a Christian just because others did it. And I have the sense that my life has been directed, or else under normal circumstances what I'm doing wouldn't make sense. I would just have gone to college four years and have come out doing what everybody else does, teach school.

"But my mother passed when I was in my second year of college and she was concerned about my finishing school before she died. So I decided to take a business course in Memphis and stayed there about nine months in general business training. My first job was working for a Baptist minister; part of the time I taught simple English to the church people.

"I worked at the Greenville Air Force Base [obvious irony here] for ten and a half years until I became dissatisfied with that. My primary reason was because I was serving in a position with a level of GS 7 but they would not assign me beyond GS 5. [She was the first Negro ever to receive a merit promotion.] They kept saying there was not enough weight in my job description for a 7, which was nonsense. So we rewrote it and added a lot more than I even carried. But I didn't get it so I quit and went to Nashville to work for Bishop Golden for a year. My husband works at the post office and he was going to transfer, but it didn't work out.

"I began to wonder there. Something didn't happen, because we had all kinds of wheels turning, and it should have come through. I was only home six weeks when the Delta Ministry got me to work with them. So when I review the events of my life, why things happen like they do, and you have this push and drive which causes you to do things—normally speaking I'm doing too much and don't do it all well—you have to think something.

"My husband says 'I know what you'll say when I ask you why you do all that you do. You'll say I do it because I've got to do it.'

"We have four children and one is going to the University of Southern Illinois this year. My second son goes to school there this fall. So that's about the size of that. It brings you up to date on where I am at at this point.

"I've been fortunate enough always to be in a position of service and I enjoy it. And I have no malice in my heart against anyone. I know everybody hasn't done like I would have liked for them to have done, and everyone has not been fair, but that shouldn't cause me not to try to be fair.

"Some of these people . . . like I spoke to some of these ministers . . . finally after two years, almost three, the white Ministerial Association invited me to talk to them about the Delta Ministry. I said I know we all have our limitations, but the thing I hold against them is getting in the way of those who can move further than they can. Do what you can; but don't get in the way of somebody else who can do more, which is what y'all've been doing."

The remarkable Mrs. Barnes, doing more, would have another addition to the way her life has been directed if she were being interviewed a year later. On June 4, 1968, she was a candidate, predictably unsuccessful, in the First Congressional District Democratic primary for Representative to the Congress of the United States. She was also a member of the Mississippi Delegation to the Democratic Convention in Chicago, August, 1968.

Isaac Foster and friend at Mt. Beulah, Mississippi.

BRUCE HILTON

Isaac Foster, director of the Poor Peoples Conference during the
move to the *land*.

The
Poor People's
Philosopher

"I've seen too many people lynched, I've seen too many people hung, I've seen too many people coldly shot down.

"It started at a very young age when my father worked for a man named Sam; I was only about six. I guess the reason I can remember it so vividly was because it involved the first black person I ever envied and desired to be like. He was a young Negro guy— I thought a man, which I judged to be anybody over 17. He came to the field with a pair of blue jeans, white socks, and pennyslipper shoes and a real cowboy hat; he had natural hair. This was the guy I envied.

"And I was chopping fast, trying to keep up with him and my mother was helping, when the boss man, Sam, got out of his truck, a battered thing. He walked over and asked the guy, 'Are you still a nigger?' (He was really a city boy from Hollandale and his father was kind of wealthy.)

"He didn't say anything. The boss man said: 'You're a smart nigger, aren't you? . . . Hmmm, I'll teach you a lesson!'

"So he walked back to his truck, got his '45' and put it, you know, in his hand naturally and walked right up to the boy, like about five feet away and said: 'You can't talk, Nigger?'

"And the guy looked up. When he did, the boss man said, 'Pow!' like that and killed him.

"I was hysterical and Mother said, 'Stop looking and go to work.'

"I've never been able to justify that, killing him like that.

"I've seen, I don't know, I couldn't count the cases of death I've seen."

We were sitting in Mr. Isaac Foster's tiny apartment, the kind of functional living space many students have in the general area just south of Columbia University in Manhattan. It was late at night and both of us had come in from separate visits to the Columbia campus; it was during the occupation of the buildings by the students in April, 1968.

I had met him two years earlier at Mt. Beulah. In the turmoil and confusion of those days, before the *peoples* went to the *land*, he stood out. Certainly for physical reasons; he's ruggedly built, handsome, rock hard at 5' 10", 200 pounds. In a business suit in New York's subways he would surely be taken for an athlete. But he stood out for many features other than his appearance.

I first met him having dinner in the community dining room with the *peoples*; we were eating ample helpings of white beans, corn bread, greens, and peaches. And he was talking angrily with friends around him, young men who had been traveling onto plantations to help awaken the workers. His irritation centered on how slowly he read; the words he spoke were forceful, tough, often the four-letter argot of the man's world, but never did they seem vulgar.

"It takes me too long to read anything. They didn't teach me right. When I got to school, I was cheated."

Foster had a high school diploma and felt this way; the average black man in Mississippi has had only six years of what passed for education. He had been reading a book that day on the guaranteed annual income, edited by Robert Theobald. It was going slowly for him but he was excited by the concept.

"Something's gotta be done to save our people; why wouldn't this work?"

One of those at the table, a student volunteer from a graduate school, talked about the book; he too thought the idea was important, commented on it, and then told Foster that he had met Theobald. He suggested that Theobald would be interested in meeting Foster. But he used several words more common to graduate school than to Mt. Beulah, and Foster interrupted him.

"What do those words mean? Talk so I can understand you, man!"

He said it without rancor, without self-consciousness. It seemed simple and correct. Of course, talk so one can understand. Don't hide behind the words that protect those who have spent their lives in schools.

And I saw him with the people; as teacher-counselor in the

classroom, as friend, as a spirit who kept hopes alive. I had watched him on the *land*, trying hard to see that something got done without dominating. And I had seen him play basketball, not his best sport, but alive with the fun of it, competitive, young. Isaac Foster, born in 1942, was 24 at the time. But he had lived a great deal.

He had remained with the people until they were on the *land*, until the *plydom* houses were up, and then he had traveled to New York in the fall of 1966 to begin, not without his own private reservations, a college education. I had seen him off and on but this was the first chance we had had to talk specifically about his life. I wanted to know about him, and I hoped it wasn't prying unfairly. On his own, against all the odds, he had proved, as many others had, the lie that "our nigras are happy like they are." Or that "uneducated, ignorant" people off the plantations could not make decisions, determine their own lives.

It was never really true, although there were reasons why even southern whites of goodwill might have thought it. The plantation black man, who had no choice but to exist with the "man," had outsmarted him by telling him, showing him, what he wanted to hear and see. Jean Genet had said the world made him a thief and that he decided to be what the world wanted. James Baldwin, in his essays, has exploded the myth into many pieces. The remarkably perceptive, funny plays by Douglas Turner Ward, *Day of Absence* and *Happy Ending*, which ran for several years in New York and were presented on the first Public Broadcasting Laboratory program, explored this theme. Blacks in the audiences, we are told, found them infinitely funnier than did whites. Ward, from south Alabama himself, knew what he was talking about.

But Isaac Foster, for reasons certainly unclear to me and perhaps even to him, would not follow this route. He "kicked against the pricks" from early days and refused to practice the double life.

The question is "why?" In a family of fourteen, he falls in the middle. None of his older brothers and sisters fought it. They simply eased out of Mississippi when they got old enough. (Perhaps equally as hard to understand is how he lived through it all. For he was, in the words of that early boss man, "a smart nigger.") Now he was in New York; the two years of school were reflected most obviously in his non-Mississippi accent; nothing phony, but his nearly flawless grammar and articulation showed the effects of hard work.

There are clues which come out of this conversation, but I have no conclusions to draw. I simply accept Isaac Foster as a complex and interesting person whom I'm pleased to have met.

"There was an old man who lived near us when we first moved with my father to the place where he was killed and he was lucky enough to have a set of twin boys, about forty-five or so. They were beautiful, real beautiful. They could run, hunt, play ball with us, and I liked all that. They were all he had. They didn't have phony straightened hair, like so many guys. Those twins went swimming in the river which ran 400 yards from our house—it wasn't a river really, but a drudge ditch with a sand bottom. The water was clear. These guys were swimming there; some hunters drove up in a jeep and got out. We all heard shots. Four years or so after that, that man was sitting on his porch and he said, 'My boys will be home.' He seemed to really believe that."

HOWELL: "You mean, they were killed at that time?"

FOSTER: "Sure, that's what happened. People don't believe that in the 1950's my brothers and I used to go hunting and we used to find dead bodies all the time, either hanging in trees, floating up to the bank, or dumped. The woods there are like solid for 100 miles, reaching from Tribbett all the way into Sunflower and running down to the gulf. They are huge. The thing was, you found a dead body and reported it, you were found dead next. Nobody was allowed to tell it. Forget it, it was no sense.

"You know the old man we were talking about earlier, who helped us out so much at the beginning? He had a son, one of three sons, conceived by a mulatto. The kid was really beautiful, between white and black. He was walking down the streets in Leland in 1952 —I think it was '52—and these 'crackers' were sitting in the car with their daughters; and the daughters looked at the man, and, like, they whispered to themselves and the men knew what their daughters were saying to themselves: 'There goes a beautiful Negro.'

"And so they got out and called the boy, followed him and told him, 'You know, you're a pretty nigger; we're going to have to do something about you, because the white girls like you.'

"That night, about 1 A.M., they were sleeping and they came and knocked and said they wanted to buy something. He opened the store and they put the guns on him and said: 'Where's that son of yours? He's too beautiful.'

"And they tied him up and went in, got his son, brought him out, before the old man, and tied the boy's hands and legs, and cut his penis and his testes all off and stuffed them down his throat before his eyes. And that was the thing that made his father somewhat radical, that made him start trying to buy land to become independent."

HOWELL: "Did he die?"

FOSTER: "No, he still lives in Greenville. . . . He's a wonder. . . . No, he didn't die.

"It's like a haunting thing that never dies. Things like that, if you see them and don't completely force them out of your mind, I don't see how a person could live without becoming radical and having the desire to get rid of this. . . ."

Foster was born on a plantation and worked on it as long as he can remember. "My father was a strong man, weighing about 180. From what I understand, he had come here from Louisiana, having been burned out; many were killed that time by nightriders, but he and some other kids escaped. He was stubborn; he didn't let a white man curse him."

He always wanted to go to school, but they were often kept out to work, orders of "the man." When he begged to go, his parents would often get mad and whip him. "But they did it out of frustration; we kids had to work, for it was work or starve. So they'd tell us harshly that 'you can't go' but we learned that they really loved us and only did it because they had to."

He began driving a tractor as early, he recalls, as eight; the most he remembers attending school before his twelfth year, when he stayed in town and drove a school bus to attend more often, was about thirty days. But even when he went to school they were plantation schools and "worse than nothing. It was all garbage except I learned a little math which I could do on my own and got to read some things.

"My family was very religious but I've never been very much

so. I think I realized where God stood when I was very young. I had cursed or something, without knowing what it meant, and my mother scolded me, telling me about God 'jurdging' and Jesus soon coming. She told me about what was wicked and what wasn't and how what I said was bad.

"She didn't make clear to me what she meant by Jesus coming, to 'jurdge' the wicked, and for three or four days, I watched for Jesus. I never saw him. I still have—right now—dreams about that thing. The dream has gone through different stages.

"I once heard a preacher lie, about Methuselah, the oldest man that ever lived. He called the children by his side and said the Lord had called him home and they put him away. I asked the preacher where he saw that in the Bible and he told me. And I went home and by the age of eighteen I had gone through the Bible twice looking for it. I saw things like Methuselah, at the age of 187, 'began' Lamech and Lamech, at 182 begets Noah. Nothing there about the death of Methuselah. Later Noah was looking for righteous people and he couldn't find them; he was told to fix the ark for the flood. And if you add Methuselah's age up, you'll find that's when he died."

Mr. Foster's father, having decided to buy some land in order to be independent, had almost completed the arrangements in 1957; the purchase would have been from a black landowner and he had just about worked out the legal details. The White Citizens Council and the Ku Klux Klan began threatening him; at that time, according to Foster, whites were buying up all available land to keep it from any Negroes with "ideas." Just before he signed the deeds in 1957, he was shot in his own home, while most of the family was within 100 yards. His nine-year-old daughter, who had heard the noise, ran to see what was happening; the killer knocked her down as he dashed out, heading for the woods.

"Within ten minutes, the sheriff showed up; now our house was way off from anywhere, with no phones, and he had to know what was going to happen. In fact it was another sheriff—never mind his name—who did it. In the papers the next day they said, 'Willie Foster from Longspur committed suicide yesterday!'

"Now he had been shot through the head with his own shotgun;

the gun was on the bed, the shell was seven or eight feet away. How the hell could it have been suicide?

"Now we all knew who it was but couldn't do nothing about it. I decided to kill the man myself, had a trap all set one day, up in a tree when he was driving down a back road, but he didn't come back the way I thought. Later I decided it would be useless to kill him because it wouldn't bring my father back.

"My father's problem was that in spite of the fact that he had courage, he kept it all in, like when they threatened him not to buy the land. But I think where he was foolish was to pray that God would help him rather than understanding that help came from his own self. He was a victim of his faith. Since his death, I had wanted to help my family and help others see the problem.

"Last summer I went to see my oldest brother, who has been living in Michigan for eleven years. I wanted to see what he was like, what we would say to each other. And it was something, just like when we were born. We weren't allowed to play with toys, have a ball, read books except the Bible, or shoot marbles. It was, according to the Bible, an idolatry, idling away the time.

"And it was the image with him; his children—he has eleven—can't have balls, read even their school books at home, shoot marbles, visit friends of a different faith. I tried not to approach him from a know-it-all level; we sat down and tried to talk. But he is very irritated about my going to school—as a matter of fact most of my older brothers and sisters are. 'If you want to learn something,' he says, 'the Bible says you learn of God.'

"And yet the Bible says, 'the beginning of knowledge is the fear of God,' and this doesn't make sense. He feels civil rights work is of the devil and now I'm proving it by going to school.

"We talked a lot about the Bible and how it was written and finally I told him, 'You need to read more than the Bible.' It made me sad to see that there was no change, just like my parents, only worse. I took his children for a walk, and they told me about their problems. 'He don't let us got no balls, Uncle Isaac, and he don't let us got no bicycles.' And so on. I felt sorry for them.

"This kind of thing has to be destroyed, the perpetuation of this; at least, children like Willie's must be given a better chance."

The day before visiting with Mr. Foster I had talked with Rev. Charles Sherrod, who has worked in the movement in southwest Georgia for eight years. And he said that the hardest thing about the movement was not being able ever to have any money with which to help his family. "That's a choice we had to make," he said.

Foster and I talked about this part of the movement for a time.

"I made my mother a promise when I was in my last year in high school: 'If you will allow the children at home to go to school, I will support you all.'

"So I had to hustle to get the money. And my mother began to change, to think it was a good thing for her children to go to school. No longer did she have the hidden reasons that she always said was simply that school was evil.

"But it's been hard since the plantation strike. The grown-up children left and some of them are making lots of money now. They did help us get a house for her to live in when she had to leave the plantation. My mother doesn't necessarily understand what's happened to her children. You know, she was thrown off welfare because of me; she told her children about what happened and they mainly wrote back and said, 'You ought to kill that boy.'

"Of course, I want to help her because I was responsible for her getting thrown off welfare. I think it was worth it in order to get the other children to school. My younger sisters are finishing high school and one's going to college. And they even have good grades, which is a switch.

"Last Christmas I sent my mother money for Christmas. I couldn't go home and I knew this would mean more to her than a gift. This is a thing I've been able to analyze. When my mother's unhappy, she writes the address, the day, then: 'Dear Isaac: Holy Greeting to you in Sweet Jesus Name. Today find me saved and sanctified with a mind to stay saved. The Lord has been blessing me; I didn't have food, I didn't have this or that and the Lord told me you were going to send a check.'

"On the other hand I can get a letter saying, 'Dear Isaac: What are you doing, boy? I'd love to see you,' and I know she's happy. But when she's unhappy, that other line never changes."

After high school, he went to work for a time at the Greenville

Mill, a textile plant, where he was paid about $1.52 an hour, high wages only in comparison to that earned by field hands. But he was there only about six months when women pickets, supported by the DM and other groups, appeared to protest hiring practices. Foster was involved in incipient organizing inside to contest the low ceiling on black advancement in the mill. In short, he was not at the mill very long.

In 1965 he returned to the plantation to help his mother and to work on farm labor organization. And it wasn't long before he was involved in the first plantation strike since the 1930's. In early June, 1965, twelve tractor drivers, the most skilled of the Delta farm hands, struck: they demanded that their wages be increased from six dollars a day for sunup to sundown work to the minimum wage. The strike alone was sufficient to have all their goods tossed out into the road and, homeless, they had to scramble to find a place to live.

Look magazine wrote:

> The strikers were throwing their small numbers into a battle that was lost before it began. Mechanization is mixing its blessings across the cotton land; machines now race where humans stooped. Andrews hired white tractor drivers almost immediately [they left almost as quickly], and the defeated withdrew to crowded tents in a close-by turnip field. With them, they took a new kind of pride that is a fringe benefit of the strike that failed. . . .
> Strike City is a chancy experiment, but it could be the nursery of an idea for Mississippi: that a Negro can climb above his past and live like a new Southerner. And what if that idea becomes epidemic?[1]

Foster worked at Strike City for a time, in close relationship with Rev. Warren McKenna of the DM staff. But tensions developed between DM and the Strike City inhabitants. "They thought I was getting paid and wasn't telling them. The reason was because transportation was very important and DM helped make a truck available. But they could only let people with driver's licenses use it, because of insurance and police; most of them at Strike City didn't have one. But they never understood why they couldn't drive it. Anyway, I finally had to leave.

"After that, I didn't go anywhere for a while. I never worked towns, but stayed on the plantations, getting people to talk about their problems. And I wound up helping to get people to the big meeting at Mt. Beulah and you know the rest.

"Of course, later on we got the Strike City people to come to the *land* to help us out. It did a lot of good there, and it may also have been good for the Strike City people because they were in a bit of a crisis. They had gone out looking for jobs, they were making nativity sets—had an order for thousands of dollars which they were in the process of accepting—when Frank Smith came. They didn't want to do it anymore because the money he promised ate away at their sense of self-sufficiency. But they gained it back after their new homes were built and Frank left. They got out of their tents and went out looking for jobs. They were choicy about them and wouldn't take just anything; they didn't accept . . . from a boss man. *And they did become independent.*"

Now he's in New York City, attending Queens College. In 1966-67 he was enrolled part-time and worked part-time; finances were only a portion of the reason. It also took time to gain confidence sufficient to be a full-time student. He is now.

"I enjoy history and literature most in school. Beginning to understand better our present day, why it's like it is. Lots of things that ought to seem new are very old to me. Coming into contact with Hobbes, Nietzsche, Ibsen, most of the better writers and philosophers, seem to speak to us today. It's good to know about the ideas which still influence our culture, our time; early Egyptians, Judaism, Hinduism, Christianity, up to the present day . . . . Machiavelli is interesting."

HOWELL: "Does he sound like a Mississippi politician?"

FOSTER: "Yeah, man! And I wrote up the visit to my brother and my professor wanted me to publish it. I don't want to yet. Someday I'm going to write about a lot of things."

HOWELL: "Weren't you an athlete? And did you know George Scott?"

FOSTER: "I think I knew him; somebody like him anyway I played baseball against. I played football, basketball, and baseball, but it was a lot easier to play baseball, attending school irregular.

I also once boxed and all this. Once I had an offer to play baseball from the Cardinals. But that wasn't what I wanted to do; that wasn't me."

HOWELL: "Now that you are going to school full-time and not working, how do you finance it?"

FOSTER: "I'm financing school with an OEO grant . . . though I'm aware that OEO finances people to get them to stop agitating."

HOWELL: "Do you really believe that? I mean, I know lots of people in Mississippi might pay your way—and that of lots of your friends—to get you out of the state. But do you really think Washington would do that?"

FOSTER: "Yes, I do. People in Mississippi and people in Washington as well would do that. But I accepted it; hell, I was going to school anyway."

HOWELL: "What will you do when you go back to Mississippi? What kind of concentration? Education? Economic development? Politics?"

FOSTER: "At the present I really don't know; it's hopeless to talk about economics really. The attitudes in the schools, the churches, must be overcome. The entire people have to do whatever is to be done. Getting people to see is the thing. The experiences I had, meetings on the plantations, other things in the movement, helped me understand that. The mere fact that they could talk about their own conditions, and once they talked about it long enough, they gained a tiny piece of insight valuable to them, something they would *die for*. When people can freely talk about their problems they will begin to see them and make their own leaders.

"That part of the movement we've got to get beyond. It helped at one time to have white people come in but that too has to pass. White people can't help it but they couldn't think but from their own way and it always came out sounding like, 'I know it all.'

"I think Mississippi is now ready for the kind of movement that lets people do it for themselves. I can get people to vote or strike but they do it because I tell them. We've got to have the kind of movement that lets people talk about the problems, discontinue the kind of school system they have, discontinue the kind of Sunday services, and discontinue the kind of weekends they have, living for the weekend."

HOWELL (later): "Could you say a little more about the Sunday services?"

FOSTER: "It's typical of a preacher on Sunday to say obey your master; and that stuff about suffering like Job; a definite absence of the here and now. And people are brainwashed completely, they have lost the meaning of progress. Progress means that you do what you want done, you don't wait on God to do it. And this bit about reward being for those who suffer the longest! You've got to change people's attitudes without destroying the hopes they have that *somebody's* concerned about them and that's God."

HOWELL: "One of the interesting things about the freedom movement was its use of church buildings and the role of the church in it. Do you think that has helped this problem?"

FOSTER: "I think the death of rights leaders had this influence. The first time people could finally say, 'No, this man wasn't called by God but he was killed, murdered, and there's no reason for it.' This really shook a lot of people, but I think it was good. Made them devise a philosophy not oriented to suffering but to survival. God hasn't just called another faithful servant home, but preachers can now say, clearly, 'They have murdered another one of God's servants!' It has a revolutionary flavor."

HOWELL: "If someone said to you, the majority of black people in Mississippi, if they had enough to eat, are happy . . . well, satisfied . . . living where they are, on the plantation, so on; what would you answer?"

FOSTER: "I might agree that a lot of them have never had the chance, the alternative, to decide whether they are happy or not. My mother, if she didn't believe in God, in going to church, couldn't live. It is because they are victims that they have accepted this, so many don't see it clearly. But one thing is sure. Their children are not going to be happy and they are not going to put up with it."

It was 2 A.M. and long past time for me to stop intruding into valuable study time. If Isaac Foster does write about the things he knows, read it!

LETTING THE WORLD
PROVIDE THE AGENDA

"I hate, I despise your feasts,
    and I take no delight in your solemn assemblies. . . .
But let justice roll down like waters,
    and righteousness like an ever-flowing stream"
                                    (Amos 5:21, 24).

MISSISSIPPI TOWNS make the familiar boast that they are communities of churchgoers and they really seem to be. On Sunday mornings the churches are full of people. In this rural state the churches, and perhaps the Masonic Lodges, are often the whole social life. Potentially no institution has more influence and uses it less than the church in Mississippi.[1]

The church in Mississippi played a principal role in the formulation of the orthodox view in the 1850's, helped stimulate secession, and sustained civilian morale during the life of the Confederacy. In the desegregation emergency after 1954, the course of the clergy has been more difficult to assess [with many individuals acting with courage], but the church as a whole has placed its banner with the status quo.[2]

> The kinds of people who came . . . who didn't know anything about us—were like the Good Samaritan. In that Bible story, the people had passed by the wounded man—like the church has passed the Negroes in Mississippi—and never taken the time to see what was going on. But these people who came to Mississippi that summer—although they were strangers—walked up to our door. They started something that no one could ever stop. . . . To me, if I had to choose today between the church and these young people—and I was brought up in the church and I'm not against the church—I'd choose these young people. They did something in Mississippi that gave us the hope that we had prayed for for so many years. We had wondered if there was anybody human enough to see us as human beings instead of animals.[3]

During that dramatic summer of 1964, *human beings* began to demand with renewed determination that the "house of the Lord" open its doors to all people. Whether to respond to this pressure—or support even more energetically the goals of the freedom movement—was essentially academic to the white churches of Mississippi. Most, racist by voted definition, planned to remain that way; other congregations had, at best, silently capitulated to the culture.

Lonely voices spoke out occasionally from isolated pulpits. The most direct clash with the prevailing societal mores came January, 1963, when twenty-eight young Methodist ministers submitted a "Born of Conviction" statement which opposed the closing of public schools, supported love of *all* men, and called for reestablishment of freedom in the pulpit. A White Citizens Council member burst into the office of one of the ministers, brandished a copy of the statement, and growled: "You've messed yourself up good, boy!"[4]

By that summer, eleven of those men either had left the state or held different positions. The Methodists alone lost sixty-eight of their seminary trained men to other states by 1964.

This only confirms the impossibility of personal bravery standing alone against a society's duplicity. Martyrdom would have been unnecessary and many of those sacrificed might still be in Mississippi if the church had fulfilled its institutional responsibilities. It made considerable difference in the lives of Episcopal clergy that the Diocese of Mississippi had called for respect for the 1954 Supreme Court decision and eventual desegregation of schools.

For every man, nevertheless, who risked his pulpit, many more became outspoken defenders of racism and scores hid silently by invoking abstract and pious clichés. One minister from a city in southwestern Mississippi, wracked by terror in 1964, pontificated: "My calling is not to preach a social gospel, but it is first and foremost a sacred gospel. I look beyond the chaos which is around us today."

Similar stories about churches are part of the shared memory of the movement. Children, attempting to enter a white church in Canton one Sunday, were knocked down the back steps while their elders were being shoved away from the front door. Inside, the congregation was intoning "Love Divine, All Loves Excelling." On the Sunday after the murders of the three civil rights workers in Philadelphia, a minister in one congregation berated the press for maligning his town; he made no comment on the local toughs prowling the streets and joking about the missing men. And everyone, but everyone, knows that "Ole" Ross Barnett has taught a Sunday school class for decades.

The Methodist and Roman Catholic distortions were made more obvious because of their deviance from their national manifestations. The Southern Baptist Church, even more the victim of its culture, did not contrast as markedly with the rest of the denomination, which the old saw says is more southern than Baptist and more Baptist than Christian.

During the continuing abdication of the white church in Mississippi, concerned churchmen from across the nation were moving from individual acts of commitment—sit-ins, freedom rides, etc.—to institutional responses to the call for support from the freedom movement in all parts of the country. The late Dr. Robert Spike recounted the stunning experience which preceded the formation of the Commission on Religion and Race of the National Council of Churches:

> In the last week of May, 1963, I attended a meeting in the Harlem YMCA that lasted most of the night. This was a week following the occasion when James Baldwin, Harry Belafonte, Kenneth Clark, and a number of other Negro leaders from various professions and jobs met with Attorney General Robert Kennedy—and both the Attorney General and this group came out of the meeting filled with dismay. The Attorney General was dumbfounded to discover the depth of hostility that existed in that group, particularly on the part of some who said that if the government of the United States would not protect them in Mississippi, then they had no intention of ever trying to protect the United States government in Cuba or anywhere else. The Attorney General was very upset by this. On the other hand, the group that met with him was dismayed and disheartened by what seemed to them to be a complete lack of appreciation for the intensity of feeling that existed in the Negro community at that time. This was just at the end of the Birmingham demonstrations when hundreds of people had gone to jail.
> A week later, this same group of people, largely gathered around James Baldwin, met with a group of us who were

leaders of various denominations and ecumenical agencies, to see what kind of communication might possibly exist with that group of people. They had been so really disheartened by their conversation with the Attorney General that they were now beginning to explore what other segments of the Establishment in this country really were feeling during this period. Through some mutual friends we arranged the meeting. . . .

All of us who were there felt that we were clean as far as our lack of prejudice was concerned. We had good records on race relations; we had fought for the right resolutions in church assemblies; we were against evil in this area. But somehow it had never come to us quite the way it came on that night. We left there about 3:00 in the morning, after the most intense kind of conversation that you can imagine, with a feeling that we had been on the other end of Nathan's finger—that is, that Baldwin and others had said to us for the first time, "You are the man!" We felt a sense of personal guilt, of personal responsibility for the denial of full justice to Negro citizens, resulting in the deterioration of relationships between the races to the place it was in the spring of 1963.

Those of us who left that place that night decided that we had to do something. . . . As it happened, the General Board of the National Council of Churches was meeting the following week. . . . The president of the Council, Dr. Irwin Miller . . . appointed a special committee which came up with a resolution to establish a special commission with power for direct action. . . .[5]

The Commission on Religion and Race (CORR), perhaps providentially established three days before the tragic murder of Medgar Evers, performed its first official act by sending representatives to the Evers' funeral. During that sad visit, a plea for help from the larger church came from Negro Christians of Mississippi. This event brought the national church and—not long after—the world church, into Mississippi.

The formation of CORR itself constituted a significant development; for the first time an ecumenical body was mandated by the individual denominations to a direct action ministry in the public sphere.

CORR found itself, within a few months of its birth, confronted with the developing plans for a massive inflow of volunteers into the state in the summer of 1964. Contrary to popular misconception, the NCC through CORR did not initiate the Mississippi Summer attack on the "closed society." But it did support the Council of Federated Organizations (COFO), organize and administer the highly publicized training session at Western College for Women, Oxford, Ohio, and call for clergy, legal, and medical volunteers to stand with the primarily student participants.

Hardly had the tense summer begun when a high-ranking Justice Department official came to members of CORR and urged them to use all their influence to keep the COFO workers out of a number of towns in the most intransigent areas of Mississippi.

The Commission's reply was reported to be: "The decision has already been made and we will support it. The church cannot say to the students: 'You go into those towns alone; we find them too dangerous.' "

While CORR's assignment included mobilizing support for important legislation, challenging the churches, and direct action in crises, the Delta Ministry—discussed for almost eighteen months before its formation September 1, 1964—was conceived as a long-term, in-depth ministry of service in the state of Mississippi. Its implementation had been delayed until September during the difficult summer months. But one thing stands clear. When the churches of these United States committed themselves to the drive for equal rights and opportunities for all people in Mississippi— against tremendous local opposition—the shape of the Delta Ministry had, in a very real sense, already been determined. Before the birth of the Delta Ministry, the church had identified with the black man in Mississippi and incurred the wrath of his oppressors.

As the Delta Ministry assumed its task in the fall of 1964, on the very day that the Mississippi Summer officially ended, it rather quickly became the most significant continuation of the momentum built up during the summer. It, also, inherited something less than the kindest wishes of the political and ecclesiastical powers of the state.

From the outset of CORR's commitment to Mississippi and from the first weeks of the Ministry's life, attacks have been leveled continually at the theological assumptions underlying the NCC presence in Mississippi. How can the church be associated with people who often resort to direct action and exacerbate personal relations? Isn't the DM more concerned about civil rights than the salvation of souls? What happened to reconciliation as the key purpose of the church in the world? How can the church take sides? Given the Ministry's own guidelines, why is there no communication between blacks and whites? Is not the church faithful only when it proclaims the gospel, educates its people, worships as a congregation, and provides direct relief? In short, isn't the Delta Ministry an aberration?

National magazines have attacked it: *Time* once said it attempted "reconciliation through anger" and in typical *Time* fashion, printed the words "the white man is your enemy" under the picture of a staff member but did not quote him to say that in the story. More important critics have raised questions of a serious nature. Further, the DM's self-understanding, tempered in the crucible of the Delta, has extremely important theological implications for the whole church.

The original action of the General Board of the NCC called the Delta Ministry to "Be the instrument to focus the concern and mobilize the resources of the churches in a ministry of service, reconciliation and social reconstruction to the persons and the society of the Delta area of the State of Mississippi."

The project was to develop along three lines:

1. A ministry of services of direct relief to relieve suffering.

2. A ministry of reconciliation and the securing of human dignity which would seek the following:

    A. the establishment of communication between the white and Negro communities;

    B. to help the people locate and train leadership;

    C. to aid the people in identifying their common problems, needs, and concerns;

    D. to develop indigenous centers in each county in the citizenship school pattern.

3. A ministry mobilizing skills, resources, and public opinion to develop an adequate base for livelihood.[6]

The most tenacious and direct criticism came, over a long period of time, from Mississippi Methodist Bishop Edward J. Pendergrass, reaching its peak during the debate in the fall of 1966 over whether the Methodist Church's Board of National Missions and Women's Division would make their first, and desperately needed, contribution to the Delta Ministry. (They did, to the tune of $100,000 for the first year.) In a paper prepared for a Delta Ministry evaluation committee and, later, to argue against its funding, Pendergrass made seven specific criticisms:

1. *There has been no effort toward reconciliation.* After pointing out that one of the stated objectives of the program was the establishment of communications between black and white communities, he charged that the lines of division had been hardened.

2. *Staff members regard the civil rights movement as war.* The Bishop felt that the staff saw the movement as a class struggle between the underprivileged Negroes and the whites and middle-class Negroes in which they would even break the law and let the ends justify the means.

3. *The program is not ecumenical in nature.* "The program does not involve church people in Mississippi." (See above, page 5.)

4. *The program is perpetuating segregation.* Both Strike City and the Freedom City directions promote segregation; experience with Indian reservations should prove that fallacious.

5. *The DM's theory of "self-determination" is an illusion.* The staff has been dishonest; "when a mass of ignorant, uneducated people are gathered together it is impossible for a decision to come from the group." Obviously, they are influenced into making the decision the staff wants.

6. *The program is contrary to the modern concept of Christian mission.* While DM claims to be an experiment in church renewal, its maintenance of isolated "compounds" and judgmental "we are the way, the truth and the light" attitude recalls blindnesses of mission strategy fifty years ago.

7. *The DM program is primarily one of political action.* Direct relief has been interpreted by the staff to mean building political pressure groups of the poor.[7]

Rev. Arthur Thomas, director of DM until September, 1966, replied in his incisive way, blunt and with a compassion born of watching people suffer:

> Five hundred thousand people. 500,000 people means one out of every four in Mississippi. Five hundred thousand people, and more, began to receive food in March of this year,

1966. *For the first time* this many people were receiving food. This fact alone, that one-fourth of the population needs and is eligible for governmental food programs and is now receiving food can validate the work of the Delta Ministry.

Did the Methodist church know there were hungry people in Mississippi? . . . We tried to tell people and get them to help. We tried churches in Mississippi. Few people would even admit or recognize that there were unfed people. . . .

Five hundred thousand people, and more. (It costs) more than twenty-five million dollars to get food to these people. Only one agency appeared to have the resources for this kind of need: the Federal Government. And the federal government was hampered in its efforts to get this food to the people because of the state of Mississippi. That non-descriptive term, the state, means people, people in places of authority. Prominent people in Mississippi did not want other people to be fed. *Where was the voice of the church?* . . .

And what now? As a result of eighteen months of work this food program is providing some people with about eight dollars of food a month. That is all. *What are the plans of the church* to augment this relief program?

These people, however, can no longer wait on the Methodist church in Mississippi. They will no longer wait for anyone. A prominent white layman said recently that there can be no change without the leadership of people like himself. Unfortunately this is not true. It is unfortunate because the church has neglected its mission. It is not true because change is occurring as a result of the leadership of these people themselves . . .[8]

At stake in that exchange is the crucial question of the role of the church. The Bishop's charges begin with the church. He says that mission starts there and fans out once certain personal conditions are put right; Thomas's position implies that the needs of the world, the identification of God's action there, determine the nature of the mission. In the first, the structure of the church precedes the task; in the second, the nature of the need determines the structure of the church's response.

This debate has often been reflected in the most common criticism of the DM; that it had failed either to be a ministry of reconciliation or communication between the two warring communities. Rarely did the criticisms reflect the study that has long gone on around the world on the difficulty of ministering both to the powerful and the powerless at the same time. Dr. Reinhold Niebuhr often spoke to this problem out of his experience as a young man in a labor-oriented congregation in Detroit's seamier days.

The Delta Ministry staff who did attempt to make contacts with the white churches suffered constant rebuffs. But one does not have to single out DM staff to make the point. Countless poignant illustrations exist of the Mississippi society turning on its own white citizens when they challenged the culture's tacit *apartheid*.

Albert (Red) Heffner, an Episcopal lay leader, and his wife, Malva, made the most cautious attempts to mediate and hold down violence during the wretched bombing days of 1964 in McComb, Mississippi. Two or three times they had conversations with white participants, primarily ordained men, in the Summer Project. Within six weeks they were forced to leave McComb for Jackson, and from there, the state. Their full story is an incredible sequence of harassment and intimidation.

Not long before they left McComb, they were hosts to Bishop Paul Moore; the only people whom they could invite to their house to meet the Bishop (known as the Big Fisherman on the COFO code that summer) were eight FBI men. And even while they were present, cars continuously circled their home.

The Heffners, it must be emphasized, were not outsiders. They certainly weren't radical. They were highly esteemed members of the community and, most important to Mississippi society, the mother and stepfather of the reigning Miss Mississippi. A sign outside the town proudly identified McComb as her home. An excerpt from Heffner's diary observed that he knew a man had to stand up for what he felt was right at some time, but he hadn't expected to stand completely alone.[9]

Such an experience has been repeated countless times, and will be relived over and over again in Mississippi's miasmic climate. A sensitive minister in the Delta, who had resisted the temptation several times to follow his colleagues to an easier assignment, stuck it out because of the great need. His careful attempts simply to be in touch with black poor in his town and his moderate calls for justice cost him his pulpit in the summer of 1967. No one in the church hierarchy came to his aid and, at this report, he has been forced to continue to work with a government poverty agency.

What then does reconciliation and communication mean in so diseased an environment? How could the DM staff possibly have identified with those in bondage and related to the prevailing community at the same time? The answer seems obvious: by selling out.

Mississippi demanded from the Delta Ministry pleasant men who would help in direct relief to the poor and mediate between the "responsible" Negroes and the good whites (*Responsible* has become almost an epithet in such situations; responsible to whom? Ah, there's the rub.) But this assumed a ministry *to* people, a relationship which the Delta Ministry controlled. And it had opted to be a ministry *with* people, committed even before its birth to the movement. It could sell out the people demanding changes, but it could not remain *with* them and not recognize that there could be no true conversation between such unequal entities. For after all, the white man knew all about the "nigra" and what he wanted. As Walker Percy, novelist and a native of Greenville, put it:

> [He] was the only white man in the entire South who did not know all there was to know about Negroes. . . . A Southerner looks at a Negro twice: once when he is a child and sees his nurse for the first time; second, when he is dying and there is a Negro with him to change his bedclothes. But he does not look at him during the sixty years in between. And so he knows as little about Negroes as he knows about Martians, less, because he knows that he does not know about Martians.[10]

Reconciliation, the breaking down of the walls that separate us from God and each other, has always been a chief tenet of the Christian faith. The death and resurrection of Jesus Christ was the terrible price God paid to reconcile man to him. But the church for some generations has turned reconciliation into a static role; to violate the passivity this implies and act "politically" would be to invite censure.

Bishop Moore, chairman of the Commission on the Delta Ministry—which oversees the work of the staff—for two years, disagreed: "We engage in a ministry of reconciliation by helping the poor to gain through self-confidence, articulateness, and power to negotiate on a basis of equality of person with the powers that be.

We feel true reconciliation between unequal and alienated groups is not possible without justice [crying peace, peace, when there is no peace]."[11]

Rev. Kenneth Dean, Director of the Mississippi Council for Human Relations and a member of a Southern Baptist church, stated: "Recognition of injustice, honest confession and definition of alienation all precede true reconciliation. Without this, there can be nothing more than paternalism and hypocrisy. These first steps are what the Delta Ministry is all about."

And Miss Marian Wright, brilliant Negro lawyer on the NAACP legal staff in Mississippi, once said: "There is more communication than ever before. We are communicating. The trouble is that they don't like what they're hearing."[12]

After the controversial events in the winter of 1966, a major evaluation of the Delta Ministry was demanded. It was clear that people in Mississippi were not the only ones to question the style of the ministry. A special committee, chaired jointly by the Hon. Brooks Hays and Dr. A. Dale Fiers, reported in May and rendered a positive judgment. It did direct the NCC to answer the charges of dishonesty—saying one thing and doing another—by making its goals so explicit that everyone would finally get the picture.

By this juncture in the life of the DM, it had become clear that beyond all the talk of the identification with one community over against another, the leadership role, and the debate about reconciliation, the real issue was the concept of mission undergirding the DM. In 1964, Art Thomas had asserted: "God created the world and put man on it. If we are stewards of that world, then our religion applies to everything we do. Politics is the way we govern ourselves in our community, and the way we govern ourselves reflects our faith."[13]

Dr. Paul Lehmann has suggested that God is acting in the world through politics, which means securing and maintaining a life that is human. ". . . politics is activity, and reflection upon activity, which aims at and analyzes what it takes to make and to keep human life human in the world . . ."[14]

The crux of the theological disagreement was whether the church should be concerned with all aspects of human life; indeed, whether the church should be concerned with all the things which make and keep life meaningful.

A special committee of the NCC fulfilled the request of the evaluation committee and restated the goals for the DM in June, 1966. (See appendix.) Taking into consideration the experience of two years and the lessons learned, the new goals affirmed the thrust of the ministry into all forms of human life and activity, but was careful to place it into context:

> But God's purpose over-arches all these realms; and for that reason we are called to summon men to know that God's kingdom is near and that they are invited to enter. To speak of the Kingdom without involving ourselves in the depths of human need is a mockery. To involve ourselves in those needs without maintaining an awareness of the Kingdom that stands behind them is shallowness. Our witness is not to men's need, but to Christ as the servant and savior of men in their needs.[15]

In a world of such general change and rapid upheaval, there exists today no consensus about any theology of mission. As uneasy as it makes most people who long for the old certainties, there is little alternative to a style of life full of ambiguity, confusion, and bewilderment.

God is forever acting in the world he created, and our theology is always changing, always in-the-making. We cannot set up propositions which tell us in advance how to respond to the mystery and hiddenness of tomorrow. "We walk by faith, not by sight, and at every moment we must speak to one another of the significance of this particular posture, this step, this gait, against the background of whatever comes to us from Scripture."[16]

Once upon a time—during the Reformation days perhaps—the nature of the church seemed fairly clear. Three functions usually identified it and, in the manner of scholars, Greek terms were used to clarify—or obfuscate, depending upon one's point of view—these "marks." There was *kerygma*, or the proclaiming of the good news, *diakonia*, service and reconciliation, and *koinonia*, or fellowship which pointed to the possibilities inherent in human community.

But we no longer have any assurance that we understand the church and its relationship to the world. "We must shake ourselves loose from the assumption that we can identify in advance the place of the church in the world and can make a definitive distinction between the church and the world."[17]

The recent studies on the missionary structures of the congregation by several groups called together by the World Council of Churches are of great help in learning to live with our uncertainties about what the church is and how it is in mission today. In keeping with the realities of the day, they give no certain and discreet "marks" of the church. Rather, they point to a process of discovery which never lends itself to frozen formulae.

Their report suggests a phrase which is already common parlance: *the world provides the agenda*. This helpful concept reminds us that any mission response must come both from the demands of the gospel and the way things are; for the most part, obedience demands listening to the world proclaim what constitutes today's faithful participation.

Such a stance dictates an audacious act, taking the risk of saying —to the best of one's ability, informed by one's faith—that God is at work in this particular way in the world. For example, many have said—the Delta Ministry among them—that God has been at work in the freedom movement. Such a claim must be tentative and devoid of self-righteousness, but, in order to act, it must be made. (And one would surely feel it less presumptuous than suggesting that God is at work most clearly in church buildings which deny entrance to a man because of color.) One way to phrase the affirmation would be: "through action, in mission, through joining with those struggling for decency, equality, and freedom, we believe we are more likely than not to be identifying ourselves with God's purpose."[18]

Such an understanding would prescribe a church less concerned with its own activities and preservation and more determined to aid its people in fulfilling their vocation in the world. In a time when traditional charities are provided by the state, the church must certainly seek to use its influence to assure just distribution. As the cybernetics revolution confronts the church, it must seek for new role definitions and more profound uses of leisure when machines begin to relieve men from traditional labor. The church must be as concerned about converting the "powers and principalities" which determine human possibility and limitation as it is about individual conversion. It must prepare people to participate responsibly in decision-making as greater centralization means greater power for fewer people. Structural forms developed in other ages must be discarded if they prohibit mission. Taboo questions must be raised bravely; if the real world crisis exists between the "haves" and the "have nots" and the widening gap between them, then it must boldly attack irrational anti-communism that prevents addressing other human issues.

Uncertain as we are about what the church looks like in today's more complex milieu, cut off from assurance that our actions are faithful, how do we know if we are part of the church in mission when we are involved in what appears to be authentic response to God's action? More directly to the point of this book, when the concept of mission of the Delta Ministry is challenged, what guidelines are there to evaluate its authenticity?

Rev. Robert Raines has wrestled with this question in his new book, *The Secular Congregation*. He describes within the church the pietist and secularist controversy; in its simplest terms, the *pietist* looks for God "primarily in the church, its Word and sacraments and communal life"; the *secularist* seeks God "primarily in the world, its words, events, and the communal life of the Nation and the nations." The *pietist* looks for continuity and thinks of God as having acted in the past; the *secularist* desires change and places God's action primarily in future terms.[19]

Raines, who suggests the need for both viewpoints, is dealing primarily with the reform of the congregation of an established ministry; the Delta Ministry, on the other hand, found little to relate to at all in traditional terms.

The WCC report wrestles with the need for some way to be accountable for the "risk" taken in opting to work in a particular mission style. Once more it is helpful and again it offers no easy assurances. But it has identified several "clues" that might help in the task of finding what might be a contemporary equivalent to the "marks" of the church. It should be noted that the report searches the world first in an attempt to see what provisional ways one might dare to say where God's action is; it had found beginning with theological or ecclesiastical formulations and then looking to the world an impossibility. Thus the writers let several situations speak to them, especially places where the church did in fact seem to be in mission, even if in unconventional ways, *letting the world provide the agenda* for the shape of the response.

They found themes which might serve as "divining rods" of God's presence and action in the world. Exploratory and open, the clues they offer give us at least one way to evaluate, however provisionally, the stewardship of the Delta Ministry.

The church, in its basic definition, is "Where two or three are gathered together in Christ's name" and surely can manifest itself in unlikely or strange ways. Most assuredly, a Protestant box or an Orthodox edifice does not contain its totality. In times past, the organized church has come dangerously close to the heresy of claiming too much for itself. "God so loved the world" (John 3:16) that he acted to redeem it; Paul affirms that "God was in Christ reconciling the world to himself" (2 Cor. 5:19). The church has a special task, as did Israel, to testify to the work of God in creating and sustaining the world. But—the report suggests—the old formulation of mission, God-Church-World, needs to be reversed: God-World-Church. This is the affirmation of the New Testament. The church is a part of that which has been redeemed and should correctly point to and celebrate Christ's presence as part of God's plan for the world, not for itself.

There is, thus, nothing sacred about the forms the church has developed; if they get in the way, obedience demands the discovery of new ways of service and proclamation.[20]

If one affirms that mission is God at work to complete his plans for his creation, then it is obvious that the church does not have a separate calling. "It is called to participate in God's mission. The missionary call is a call for participation."[21]

Conversion, as an example, traditionally is identified with God's mission, but it has too often meant only the individual act, the "turning around" (or away). It is, in fact, an individual act, but it is more than that; it is, indeed, the denial of the old way of viewing the world, but it is more than that. For it is also a turning back to the world, with a new vision, a new hope; it, of necessity, forces a confrontation with the powers which corrupt and destroy one's neighbor. In short, conversion includes a sense both of eternal salvation and historical salvation, the life to come and the kingdom of God on earth.

Rev. Wayne Hartmire of the California Migrant Ministry, long associated with the battle for justice symbolized by Delano, offers a penetrating insight into the dilemma of the church when it places the personal over the corporate, charity over justice:

> The present situation (with the farm workers of California) poses a difficult problem for the churches. Charitable services, long the mainstay of Protestant penetration into poverty areas, are now problematic. The expectations of low-income people are revolutionary and not evolutionary. They want justice now and not special services for an unjust interim. Farm workers want to be organized so they can have enough power to change their situation. They will not for long tolerate programs that either evade the issue of power or get in the way of organizing.
>
> But this new situation is also *an opportunity for the churches.* English classes, health education, child care, etc., in the labor camps will now be carried on by public programs under the Economic Opportunity Act; these public penetrations are not likely to be revolutionary in focus. City Hall, public agencies, and most social welfare groups are more interested in keeping the people pacified with partial measures than in upheaval.
>
> Churchmen could lead the way in approaching the underlying social, economic, and political issues. . . .
>
> If this is an accurate analysis of the way things are, our first task is to deal with that basic relationship, i.e. with the structural evils that continue our inhumanity to our fellow men. It is dishonest to evade the structural issues and carry ameliorative programs into the camps. Our consciences may be salved, but the people are not fooled; and our efforts are neutralized by continued exploitation.[22]

A noted speaker recently said that preaching the gospel to a hungry man without offering him food is both futile and cruel.

All of this points to the basic question before us today; what does the church mean when it speaks of the *true* man? The coming of Jesus as the long-awaited Christ defines the clearest perception of what it involves to be human. His coming brings liberty and sight and good news and freedom. The goal of our participation in mission today is the revealing of Jesus as the fullest understanding of the nature of man: in short, *humanization*, offered both to man personally and in his institutions.

The University Christian Movement suggested in a study paper its understanding of what humanization implies.

> The hope we possess by faith is grounded in an understanding of Christ as one who encountered forces of dehumanization in the society of his own people, who acted and who died as one who lived freely and responsibly within that society. In so doing he brought forth a new order of life, which was realized in that community of men and women who were free to fulfill one another's needs and to represent Christ within an alien world.
>
> The fulfillment of the new order of life was never complete —nor is it today. The church has always lived with an imperative to press toward the mark of fulfilling its vision, for its own members, and for all mankind. We express that vision in terms that are most meaningful to us when we speak of spending ourselves in the creation of a more human society.[23]

Finally, it seems obvious that God, at work in all areas in the world, calls the church to participate in a variety of ways; there is no single form of response to his activity. One central parish might contain several structures; a community where people live in permanent discovery; a family-type structure, something like the current residential congregation; a "permanent availability" institution, where long-range problems can be dealt with, such as legal aid, child care, narcotics addiction, etc.; and special task forces, often on issues such as urban concerns, the social revolution, responsible investment procedures, university reform, or the communications revolution.

The Delta Ministry had a long-range assignment in a particular geographical area; the Commission on Religion and Race, a complementary one to the whole freedom movement. It may be that there should have been or may yet be a ministry specifically to the white community as it grows more open to change in Mississippi.

If the aims of the Delta Ministry in humanization are to un-shackle those without power so that they can participate fully in the kinds of social and political decisions which shape their lives, certain theological assumptions are apparent. The movement, and the Delta Ministry with it, have opted for full democracy—letting the people decide.

There are at least three suppositions which come quickly to mind:

1. To assert the importance of the individual, no matter who he is, relates to the traditional concept of man having been created in the image of God.

2. Skepticism about uncritical acceptance of any leader or any group reflects a healthy understanding of the doctrine of sin.

3. To claim that the full and equal participation of all people will produce viable decisions and not end in complete confusion might well relate to the idea of divine grace, the continuing visitation of the spirit, etc.[24]

The gospel of Jesus Christ is all about freedom, understood most profoundly. Men and movements are never free from pettiness, selfishness, and pride. But allegiance to Jesus Christ promises in-dividuals and society the eventual transcendence of those things which limit freedom. In the human rights movement, both here and all over the world, the goal has been to free all men; both the oppressor and the oppressed have been victimized, put into bond-age to the chains of discrimination, and both have had their human-ness diminished.

Many would dare say that the movement, as they have ex-perienced it, has been God's action to shatter those manacles. The national and world church, through the Delta Ministry, has *let the world provide the agenda*, and attempted to participate faithfully in God's work.

The results in the white community in Mississippi have been difficult to analyze. Those who accuse the movement and the Delta Ministry of causing a more intense reaction and increased polariza-tion are correct. But that does not invalidate the ministry; many affirm that such tension marks the prologue to a more just society in which the *dream* of Martin Luther King, Jr., might yet become reality. Segments of the white church in Mississippi have been simultaneously forced and allowed to move more vigorously into a ministry which at least recognizes the historical needs of people.

To the black community the movement has been a sign of hope and the beginning of a new day. The black church, which has also been a victim of the "closed society," has been pushed by the movement—beginning with the use of the church buildings as the only sanctuary for community meetings—toward a frontline role in demanding the new humanity.

Rev. Solomon Gort of the DM staff—himself a Negro Baptist minister who has returned to Mississippi after seminary training on the west coast—suggests: "The Delta Ministry at its inception sought to relate to both black and white churchmen. The black church saw the need for the Delta Ministry, but out of apathy and fear of intimidation gave little response. The white church which has for so long taken pride in its Biblical heritage . . . void of Negro involvement, stood in religious schizophrenia."[25]

The Delta Ministry will continue to deserve close attention and support as a remarkable illustration—one of many around the world —of what response to God's action demands.

It also needs and desires constant, concerned evaluation of its theological (and pragmatic) assumptions. The Ministry—of men and of the world—participates also in the sinfulness of us all and must be held accountable to the life and teachings of Jesus Christ by those seeking authentic mission response. Quite clearly those with whom it works judge it daily, much more for what it does and is than for what it says.

A member of the Poor Peoples Conference puts together a manger set in one of the Freedomcrafts workshops of the Delta Ministry.

KEN THOMPSON

OUTSIDE AGITATORS

WCC! Ominous initials indeed! Ask a Mississippian what they stand for and the reply most likely would be, "White Citizens Council."

How ironic then that WCC also symbolizes, in contrast to the Citizens Council perversion of human nature, the tremendously important involvement of the World Council of Churches (WCC) in the freedom struggles in Mississippi.

When the American churches began to face the intransigent problems of racism, they felt the need for support and concern from a larger context. Overseas leaders were first alerted to the possibility of a direct request by Robert Spike when he attended a conference of world religions in Mexico City in the summer of 1963. He made it quite clear that the wisdom was needed of those who had long been working in areas of tension in other parts of the world. The totality of the church had to be engaged in this crisis, one of the crucial foci for the world church in the past few years.

Thus, for the first time in the history of the ecumenical movement, the United States of America requested special consideration from the whole of the church. It marked an extremely important moment; to bring this to the attention of the rest of the world constituted a confession, an admission, that in spite of the enormous material wealth of the U.S. church, it was psychologically and spiritually unable to confront the racial crisis in isolation. For almost two centuries, the church of the United States had viewed itself as a "giver" of people and funds to other lands. To be a recipient was a new and significant experience.

Sharing of the experience, enlarging the fabric of involvement, and honest confession probably motivated the original request for aid from the Division of Inter-Church Aid, Refugee and World Service (DICARWS, the WCC Division involved). But it is equally clear that the substantial amounts of money made available for the Delta Ministry have prevented premature death more than once.

The dollars and cents totals are significant; from 1965-68, regular donations to the Delta Ministry have approached $300,000, about 25 percent of the budget of the DM during that time. Even more impressive are some of the sources of those gifts; during a dreadful famine, the National Christian Council of India sent $211; the Evangelical Church of Cameroons, $686; the East Asia "Least Coin" fund added $1,000; and, most unexpected, the tiny but liberal Christian Council of South Africa donated $280.[1]

Dr. Geoffrey Murray, Information Officer of the Division of Inter-Church Aid, Refugee and World Service, wrote: "These relatively small gifts express the concern and solidarity of struggling indigenous churches which have themselves to seek ecumenical support for their projects."[2]

Following the assassination of Martin Luther King, Jr., a special memorial fund in his name totalling more than $100,000 was channeled into the Delta Ministry by DICARWS. Large amounts came from the more affluent countries of Europe; again, one was touched by a gift of at least $200 from Kenya.

And money begets money. It stands to reason that the faith placed in the project by the WCC made it more mandatory that domestic church bodies stand behind the ministry, especially with their contributions.

Such continuing involvement calls for an expression of gratitude from those who benefit from another's largess. A startling reversal of the traditional mode of native appreciation was staged in Washington, D.C., February 6, 1967.

> On that day the natives of darkest America sent to the enlightened Christians of Africa a token of gratitude for their aid in the rescue of their mission to Mississippi. It was a most fitting token too, a cross of light oak and dark hickory, beautifully laminated and finished by unskilled black hands in the heart of America's color jungle, a mission known as Freedom City, near Greenville, Mississippi. It was the kind of token American missionaries used to send back from Africa to their American churches.[3]

The late Dr. Z. K. Matthews, first ambassador to the U.S. and the U.N. from Botswana and an ecumenical leader, was commissioned to carry the cross back to Africa, along with this message from Mr. Owen Brooks, acting director of the DM, who presented the cross: "Without the concern of the people overseas, including those in Africa and Asia, our work might have ended in 1965. Your help came at a most critical time."[4]

The first official presentation to the DICARWS about support of the Delta Ministry had been in Geneva, Switzerland, May 4-5, 1964, while DM was still in the planning stage and immediately before the Mississippi Summer Project. It was not insignificant that Dr. Eugene Carson Blake, now General Secretary of the WCC, presided at this meeting as chairman of DICARWS. His own involvement in the freedom movement was well known; he reported that the discussions within the NCC had led to a "considerable amount of soul-searching on the part of the NCC about this action since it was not their normal pattern to expect help as directly as this."

The proposal itself, he pointed out, explained "why this was a proper request, and the overwhelming vote of representatives of the churches in membership of the NCC was to ask for this assistance."[5]

Dr. W. A. Visser 'tHooft, then General Secretary of the WCC, responded that "this was the first project from the U.S.A. to appear before DICARWS in the history of its work. There is something very impressive about this request. It was a manifestation of keen ecumenical consciousness and Christian humility."[6]

As a result, the Delta Ministry was listed in the 1965 project list, circulated to the total membership of the WCC during the fall of 1964, and it has reappeared each succeeding year. DICARWS reevaluates its projects after five years.

Although the original request stressed the help of persons who had had experience in areas of tension and social change at least as emphatically as financial aid, this aspect of the relationship has been somewhat less satisfactory. A significant number of churchmen from other countries have visited "the work" in Mississippi, and the dialogue between those in staff assignments and the visitors proved extremely valuable. But there has been only one direct assignment to the staff of the ministry of a "missionary" from another country. His own experience had not, in fact, prepared him for the pressures of Mississippi, and he left the U.S. a somewhat embittered man. One or two nominees have not, for one reason or another, been accepted by the staff in Mississippi.

Interestingly enough, however, several international persons have heard about the ministry on their own and made their way to Mississippi to serve as volunteers with the ministry and in almost every case a mutually satisfactory involvement resulted.

One important ecumenical visitor, Miss Janet Lacey (important because she helped raise funds for the DM as Director of Christian Aid for the British Council of Churches, and, in some circles, famous as the first woman ever to preach from the pulpit of St. Paul's in London) reported:

> I sat in small shops and houses and listened to tragic stories told in a language Shakespearian in style, and I cannot find words to describe their courtesy and dignity as they spoke of their Christian faith and their struggle for social justice . . . The project must go on and we must all help. It is ecumenical, it is the church in the front line, and it is about human suffering borne with courage and good humour. The greatest task for all is reconciliation between peoples. They are afraid of each other. Just now the whites think that if only the outsiders would go away the Negroes would return to their happy acceptance of a former life.They find it hard to recognize that this is not possible. Integration is a two way operation, and there is a great need for pastoral care for both communities. The member churches of the WCC must see this project as their responsibility as well as of the American churches. Some of the aspects of race prejudice are equally bad in Great Britain and must be resisted.[7]

The response of others in the world church indicates that they too found the new relationship with the U.S. church to be meaningful. Dr. Christian Berg of Germany said: "Christians in other countries might learn a great deal from the fact that churches in a giving country needed ecumenical help."[8]

Bishop Lesslie Newbigin, then on the WCC staff, wrote: "Those of us who have benefitted for so long from the generosity of the American churches are grateful for the fact that the NCC has been ready to do something which required even more than generosity, namely the grace to ask for help. We are glad to be invited."[9]

Not the least of the benefits to the American churches was some negative experience in what it meant to receive aid. As an example, one large sum was announced through the WCC offices and the press release indicated that the money would be spent on a particular project with the Delta Ministry selected in "consultation with the staff." All of those with responsibilities for the DM stated that no one had contacted any of them and, further, they thought there were higher priorities on the use of the money than that indicated. The matter was cleared up rather easily, but the object lesson was not lost on those who usually give.

Another time a talented couple visited with the staff to discuss joining the ministry. Although they were gifted, the staff felt to a person that their style was much more suited to a classroom or other more structured situation. "Things are too delicate here to allow whites who carry authority in every word they speak to work with developing blacks," reported one of those who had made the difficult decision. There is little question that the judgment was correct; but surely the American church has to ask itself, "When was the last time a church to whom we were sending missionaries had the freedom to ask them not to remain?"

Not the least of the achievements of the Delta Ministry has been its remarkable indigenization. In September, 1964, the ministry was essentially five white ministers, four men and one woman, all from outside the state, attempting to find channels to be effective.

By June, 1968, the staff—still consciously integrated—nevertheless had black citizens of Mississippi in all the key leadership roles, both administration and field projects. On a staff of thirty-two, only six are originally from outside the state and five have been in Mississippi two or more years. Four whites remain. Since the summer of 1966, the white staff served primarily in support roles, such as office administration, interpretation outside the state, coordination of volunteers, and bookkeeping. This has had the side effect of defusing some of the hostility toward "outsiders," however dishonest that was, and larger numbers of whites in Mississippi have begun to hear the Delta Ministry "tell it like it is."

Dr. T. Watson Street, executive secretary of the Board of World Missions, Presbyterian Church U.S., made some provocative suggestions for what southerners might learn about mission from their reaction to the DM.

"American churches have been accustomed to sending missionaries (agricultural, educational, etc.) to lands around the world. Now churches around the world will show that missions are no one-way street, that all churches must be ready to receive as well as to give, that missionaries from overseas are able . . . to help churches of the United States. . . ." Among the lessons for a southern Christian:

1. To understand what it means to receive rather than to give. One who resents "outside agitators" in spite of obvious needs, might begin to understand why people in "mission" lands have not always appeared "properly grateful" for our presence.

2. To comprehend how humiliating publicity of weaknesses can be. These same "outsiders" tell people in other parts of the nation and around the world of discrimination and poverty which exist at home. "Whatever we think of the situation in the South, we can better understand how painful it is for a national Christian to hear presented the weaknesses of his land."

3. To grasp the importance of the "new mission" approach overseas. Dr. Street suggested that the "failure" of the DM to work with the churches of Mississippi violated the "new mission" rubric of never going into a project over the heads of the local church. The lesson is well intended, even if Dr. Street repeated the error of equating the church and the "white" church as one and the same in Mississippi.[10]

The precedent-establishing experience of the Delta Ministry in admitting its need for broad support surely will be repeated increasingly in the years ahead.

The Commission on Ecumenical Mission and Relation, United Presbyterian Church, U.S.A., asked a number of experienced personnel from other churches to participate in its "crisis in the nation" program in the summer and fall of 1968.

Since the time of St. Paul, those notorious "outside agitators" called Christians have stuck their noses into the business of others.

It upsets Mississippi politicians who argue that such outsiders are probably "reds." If the United States is ever to be shaken from its complacency about the overwhelming problems of hunger on a world scale, if it is ever to see itself and the rest of the developed nations as the "problem" for the developing countries, surely it will take the most sensitive and persistent effort on the part of the world church and its kind of agitator. They have a lot to give; we have a lot to receive.

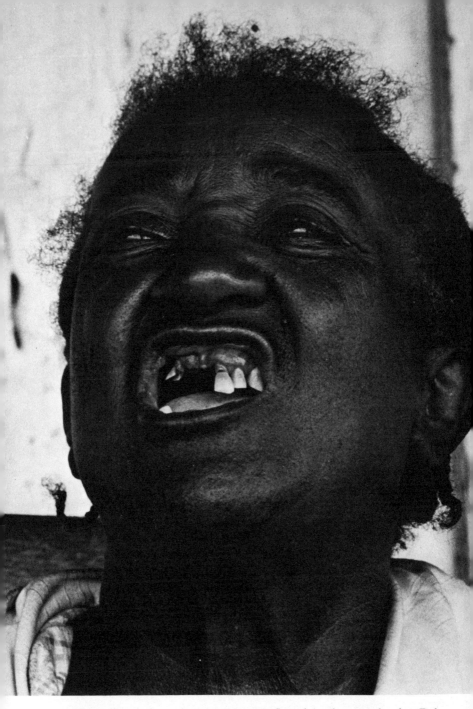

Poor diet and no dental care are reflected in these teeth of a Delta woman.

AL CLAYTON

IN THIS CROESUS
OF A NATION

SARGENT SHRIVER, speaking on television in 1968, said: "If
we devote that kind of money to it, let's say half of what we're
putting into Vietnam, we can eliminate poverty in this nation,
poverty defined in terms that we have defined it, in accordance with
income, food intake, housing, education, and so on. We can eliminate it. The question is not whether we can; the question is: will
we, do we have the will power to do it, do we have the motivation
to do it?"[1]

In Sunflower County, Mississippi, 1966, the Federal Government spent $10,200,000 on "welfare" to planters; it was able to
scrape together $446,000 for food programs.

Sen. James Eastland, whose home is in this county and who
represents in his "good offices" the needs of one of the poorest
sections of the United States, received $157,390 in 1967 for not
planting cotton. His 5,800 acres of rich cotton land, which would
bring between $400-$500 per acre, is appraised at the tax assessor's
office at $18,200, or an average of $3.14 per acre. His personal
property evaluation—including all the expensive farm machinery—
is $750. He paid an average of 29 cents an hour to adults and 21
cents to children during the 1967 chopping and picking season.[2]

Poor Americans, according to statistics, are four times as likely
to die before the age of thirty-five as the average citizen. Negro
women in Mississippi die six times as often in childbirth as white
women. The life expectancy of the American Negro at birth is 61;
that of a white American, 68.

Poor women in general have no prenatal care; 45 percent of the
mothers in public maternity wards have had no such care, and most
black mothers in the Delta never reach the hospital for delivery.

This deprivation makes it three times as likely that a child will
be born prematurely, and mental retardation is ten times more
likely in very small premature babies than those born at full term.
In 1940 the infant mortality rate for non-whites was 70 percent

higher than for whites; in 1962, the gap had actually increased to 90 percent.

Such a list could be extended indefinitely. Let it suffice to repeat that in Mississippi we have only the tumor of our national disease which is easiest to detect. Robert Sherrill points to the shape of our failure:

> Apparently the feeling in Washington is that enough has already been done for the southern Negro; the White House Civil Rights Conference of 1966 was aimed almost entirely at smothering the ghetto blazes of the North. A Mississippi sharecropper I met at that conference suggested with the mildness that is typical of these stoical, forgotten people, "If the politicians mean to help me, why don't they quit politickin' and *do.*" None of the vaunted civil rights laws of the middle 1960's have touched his life. Probably none ever will. Having been evicted from his land by the white owner because he tried to send his children to an integrated school, he now farms five acres which he rents from a friendly black man and tries to raise a family of six children on less than $2,000 a year (which makes him one of the more prosperous blacks in Mississippi, as a matter of fact). There are millions like him in the Deep South. The federal government has worked no miracles for them; it has not even worked a change.[3]

The same writer reported in the *New York Times Magazine,* June 4, 1967, that "It Isn't True That Nobody Starves in America." This article, coupled with the report already mentioned by the doctors' committee on starvation in the Delta, caused a storm of reaction. Many southern politicians denied the charges, but Sen. John Stennis, who was among those discounting the findings, nevertheless proposed $75,000,000 in emergency food distribution if there were hunger and pushed it through the Senate.

The legislation died in the House. Sherrill reports:

> Southern congressmen got the blame, and it is true that many of them did oppose the emergency food program; but it was killed not so much by their axes as by the chloroform of an indifferent Administration, which—to save money for Vietnam—withheld its support. The national mood had been perfect for reform. . . . but . . .[4]

Enterprising reporter James Batten discovered in late 1967 a major report by the President's National Advisory Commission on Rural Poverty called "The People Left Behind." The thrust of the report, now widely available, is that federal policy has systematically short-changed rural America, leaving 14,000,000 people consigned to deprivation and hardship. The commission warned that this situation must be remedied before the current battle to save the nation's cities could ever make sense. But the White House had refused to release the report until Batten uncovered it; apparently the Administration did not want to jeopardize programs it was already having difficulty funding.[5]

It is in the light of Mississippi's xenophobia and callous disregard of one whole segment of its people—and in face of the nation's abdication of its responsibilities[6]—that the work of the Delta Ministry must be viewed.

In 1966, an editorial critical of the DM appeared in a Mississippi newspaper, repeating the old cliché, "Where there's been that much smoke, there's bound to be a little fire."

It has been noted by those schooled in logic that when there is smoke we are certain only that we shall find smoke. A friend, discouraged after reading many finely tuned statements by church organizations that resulted in no visible action, felt that where there is an excess of "holy smoke" one had better beware of smoke screens.

Perhaps he would be gratified to know that behind the Delta Ministry's smoke there has been some of the fire so desperately needed.

The evaluation committee which had studied the ministry in 1966 (and which many feared was a tactic to curtail or kill the program) gave a resounding endorsement to it. In a key paragraph, the report stated:

> The Delta Ministry has become the number one civil rights organization in Mississippi; it has been the best financed; has produced results far beyond the gross activity of other civil rights groups. It has brought hope to the poor Negro in Mississippi for whom the NAACP, the church, the Federal Government and the local governments had offered no hope. It has

caused commodity relief to be distributed in counties where it had not been distributed [$24 million worth for 200,000 persons]; it brought into being organizations which have Head Start Programs [with more than $7 million in less than a calendar year to be spent in Mississippi]; it has kept the pressure on the Federal and State power establishments in such a way that they have had to act responsibly in the arena of civil rights, relief, and to a degree, in education. They have served as a corrective to "administrative lawmakers," i.e., OEO officials who would have set "separate but equal" programs or possibly all white programs to the exclusion of Negroes and as a corrective to State and City officials who might have otherwise ignored the poor Negroes. To the degree that they have focused national attention on the problems of the poor, they have helped poor people all over the country. They have developed models of hope-producing organization for the poor which will be copied in many parts of the country, if not the world.[7]

Harvey Cox, noted theologian, has written:

> In an age when the Church has compromised itself with property, power and prestige, the Delta Ministry works among the poor, the wretched and the disinherited. My own experience in the racially troubled Southland and in the explosive Northern urban ghettos has convinced me that we need a dozen more ventures like the Delta Ministry.
>
> Of course, its work will be misunderstood by those who see the Church as an arbiter rather than as a prophet and protagonist. It will be criticized by those who want it to "go slow," to stand always for order, even against justice.
>
> I may differ with individual decisions the Delta Ministry makes, but I trust the judgment of its experienced, dedicated staff.
>
> For me, the DM is one evidence that God may not be as dead as some people think.[8]

Such positive evaluations of the Ministry, even with other specific criticisms, especially by the evaluation team, ended the public debate about the efficacy of the church's involvement in Mississippi. But it did not end attempts by a few to cut back its effectiveness by pushing hard on the question of financial integrity while at the same time trying to keep money out of the Delta Ministry budget.

Now the nature of the involvement has changed as the emotional heyday of the civil rights movement has passed and longer-range issues have become the heart and soul of the DM's efforts. Its work has been less spectacular, but certainly no less difficult; and as almost all the key posts have come to be held by native Mississippians, the criticisms have had to be more specific also.

Hodding Carter, III, once widely quoted to blast the Ministry, wrote an article in the *New York Times Magazine* in March, 1968, in which he cited several small signs of hope in the Delta. Three of those projects were related to the Delta Ministry, and he quoted —favorably—three DM staff.

Time magazine, in a cover story on poverty May 17, 1968 (almost surely inspired by the much-discussed presence of thousands of poor at Resurrection City in Washington), for the first time said something positive about the Delta Ministry:

> . . . another cotton chopper named Walter Abney, 35, has eluded the grip of The Man. Working the same hours for the same wages as Perkins, Abney was spared the burden of children; two years ago, the Delta Ministry . . . set up Freedom City near Greenville, Mississippi, and Walter signed on. Now he and his wife live in a rent-free, two-room apartment with a somewhat leakproof roof, and receive $30 a week of *deus ex machina* handouts. Walter Abney is free of The Man.[9]

This, and similar comments, indicate that the DM has won its battle with the establishment critics and reassured its sometimes worried friends; it has been given the right to exist, even if primary interest has shifted elsewhere.

Dr. Jon Regier, head of the Division of Christian Life and Mission, National Council of Churches, who has worked long and hard to win ideological and financial battles on behalf of the Delta Ministry, feels that the "original commitment to a long-term mission enterprise is still legitimate. Some of the things it had done can and should be picked up by local efforts. But the fundamental task of community development still has a substantial amount of work left to be done and will require a broad-based drive from within and without the state. Though progress has been made in Mississippi, the basic task of building a just society is far from being completed."

The appointment of Rev. Andrew Young, executive vice president of the Southern Christian Leadership Conference, as chairman of the Commission on the Delta Ministry, that group with oversight of the fieldwork of the Ministry, in May, 1968, further guaranteed the acceptance of the Ministry and its continued relevance.

But the true validation, the real significance, of the Ministry does not finally rest upon the goodwill of the many church boards or the uneasy co-existence with the powers-that-be in Mississippi.

That will come from those with whom it has worked and will rest with its "doing" rather than its "saying."

What it is going to do was pointed to in the following interview with Owen Brooks, who has been with the staff since 1965 and is now the director of the DM.

Lean and intense, Brooks had left a profitable job as an electrical engineer in Roxbury, the black ghetto of Boston, to come to Mississippi. Although he was well-known locally for his work in voter registration in Bolivar County, he reached the public eye as a key figure on the Meredith march, where he was a tireless participant both on the march and in the strategy sessions that changed the nature of the march to encourage voter registration.

His friends and his critics (and no one could have this job without the latter) point to one primary characteristic that marks him: his single-mindedness. His strength is in work in the field, concentrating in Cleveland, where he lives, driving at some time in almost every day to the DM office at Greenville, 37 miles away.

In conversations with Brooks, certain notes which help point to where the DM is headed, emerged.

Howell: "Perhaps if you give me a few examples of the kind of work you and others on the staff do in Cleveland, it would help me understand what the DM is doing in its longer-range involvement."

Brooks: "We've been involved in all areas of community development, voter registration, citizenship education, and basic political organization, particularly around the campaigns of 1965-68. We've also worked hard to assist independent poverty programs, separate from the many community agencies controlled by the state and used as a pressure to keep people in line. Other programs have spun off these basic directions.

"For example, we assisted in the organization of a community hospital after bringing Mound Bayou and the Cleveland Negro hospitals together. It took hard-nosed effort to get open elections to the board of directors of the hospital. We've been involved with the Tuft's medical program to children, but there've been some problems there. They don't want to let the local people have enough say on their boards.

"We've done food and clothes distribution. We've had to work both to fight the wrongs in the food programs and to help people understand the use of things like food stamps. And we're always hassling with the welfare department, keeping community pressure on. So far, our best way to keep people informed and involved still is the community gathering. And one of the things we've got to do more with is youth. They're angry all over Mississippi and rightly so. Anyway, we consider ourselves interested in and want to be as active as possible in all areas that affect the lives of people."

Howell: "Freedom City took a lot of staff energy in 1966. How does it fit in these days and do you think it gives promise now of being a viable community?"

Brooks: "It did take a lot of staff time then, and still indirectly diverts funds from our budget, though most of the money raised for it hasn't shown in our budget. It began to be much more independent by mid-way in 1967 and is even more so now that it has the Ford and OEO grants; the Delta Opportunities Corporation has taken over most of the administration. The real breakthrough came in the spring of 1967 when the people began to work with the surrounding community on voter registration. They would go out and those in the community would come into Freedom City."

Howell: "Mr. Jake Ayres (who runs the Freedomcrafts program) told me that the poverty money which has come in, like everything else here, has not helped the real poor. Do you agree?"

Brooks: "In most ways, that's accurate. Poverty money too often has been put into the hands of the power structure, and is controlled either directly or indirectly. It has scarcely had maximum participation of the poor.

"But gains have been made in certain areas. Compared to the numbers involved when I first got here, there is a great deal of new involvement of people in community affairs. There are great gains in enfranchisement. And many are involved in various community organizing projects. So, although it's not enough, many people have been helped to do some constructive things because of poverty money help. And I think the numbers will continue to grow."

HOWELL: "Do you see any hopeful economic signs, such as industrial developments which would get at the employment problems?"

BROOKS: "The picture is bleak. So much hinges on the direction the federal government takes, and the Vietnamese war has squelched serious efforts there. Trying to bring Mississippi and the other isolated areas into the mainstream is a difficult task. And politically we are in bad shape in getting the government to accept its responsibilities for the eradication of poverty. Washington is not without some good people who would like to do more imaginative and daring things, but I don't think they'll be able to buck the tide."

HOWELL: "What is the biggest problem facing the DM?"

BROOKS: "You know that we consider ourselves to be involved in a long-term ministry. Frankly, I expect a recession of the support for us, personally and financially, given the temper of the country. We'll have to fight to hold the line. There's a tremendous reaction on the part of the conservatives all over which will make it difficult to hold the line. And we've got to tackle increasingly subtle problems here in Mississippi."

So has the church and the nation. If we can, in the words of Sargent Shriver, eliminate poverty with the proper will, then there is no excuse either for the church or the nation for a failure to do it.

It is really a matter of priorities. In an extraordinary report entitled, "Poverty In the Rural South," Paul Good says bluntly:

> Last year, circumstances called attention to poor conditions in Mississippi, and the country at large was made aware that in this Croesus of a nation black children went to bed hungry and woke up sick to live or die as best they could. The country had been unaware. It could sight a landing space on the moon, but it could not see a shack in the Delta. It could bounce TV shows off a satellite but it could not hear a man on earth plead for work. It could spend $800 million a year on food and clothing for its dogs and cats while children cried for milk and shoes.[10]

The Delta Ministry has made its mistakes and failed to be all it should be at times and places. More important is to find what in it calls us all to account for the ways we spend our time and our energy, for the ways we rationalize discrimination and hunger, for our apathy in the face of suffering, for our willful ignorance as human beings are destroyed..

The Delta Ministry and all those with whom it works demand a response that the late Sen. Robert F. Kennedy often used: "Some men see things as they are and say, Why? . . . I dream things that never were and say, Why not?"

Human instincts demand more from our nation than it has been ready to give. Self-preservation dictates more from our nation than it has wanted to do.

It is time for the whole church to speak out as unambiguously as has the Delta Ministry.

The *land*.

NASH BASOM

Appendix

THE GOALS OF THE DELTA MINISTRY

I. Work with the Dispossessed

We believe that in the work which has priority—the work with the dispossessed—the goals can be usefully summarized under four headings.

1. *Immediate Human Needs*

From the beginning, the concerns for the elementary human necessities—food, shelter, clothing—have been the concerns of the Delta Ministry. These will continue to be central; but wherever possible, the concern must be to bring the necessary pressure upon agencies to accept this as their proper responsibility. In emergencies, direct action to relieve need may be unavoidable; but normally (in the face of the enormity of the need and the limited resources of the Ministry) it is important to keep out of the welfare business and to press the governments concerned to the point where they are forced to meet the immediate needs.

2. *Economic Development*

The path of escape from social bondage for the Negroes of the Mississippi Delta includes closing the educational gap, and overcoming political exclusion, and to these the Ministry must address itself. But it is possible to be educated, politically emancipated citizens, and still to have no access to the world of economic opportunity. The term "opportunity systems" is sometimes used today to describe the necessity for planning the path to final freedom in such a way that the total pattern of exclusion may be overcome. Exclusion is a total system. So must the plan for opportunity be total. Nothing less will suffice, in the end, than an "opportunity system" which opens the job market, the capital pool, the management doors, along with the educational systems, the housing and social worlds, and the political arenas.

For this reason the Delta Ministry has found itself inevitably driven on from its earliest welfare, education and voting rights concerns, towards economic development programs, including the projected "model" development of a "New Community" in which the dispossessed will learn how to enter the world of economic opportunity by independent, cooperative planning and action, establishing political, social, and economic institutions which the poor community itself administers and controls. This must not be a proposal for self-sufficiency—a separate black nation; but it is a proposal for self-determination—through learning the meaning of social and political power in such a way that the poor will learn how to enter the world of equal opportunity as a partner and not an inferior. Help will need to be given from "outside" but the answers must grow from within, as the poor person emerges from the state where he is a dependent for whom others plan and provide.

The resources for reaching these objectives are not in the churches' hands. For this reason the churches through their Delta Ministry can seek only to be a catalyst, working with and through government and other agencies toward these objectives. The timetable for the development of communities of self-responsibility and for emergence from experienced power by the Negro community into the situation where there is "neither black nor white" cannot be set in advance. The goal can be set as equal economic opportunity in an open society; the timetable remains open.

3. *Public Responsibility*

Voter registration will continue to be a vital aim. And beyond that, the emergence of an informed and responsible electorate. In the immediate future this process seems destined to produce major conflict concerning the way to a responsible electorate. We affirm the necessity for free participation by all in the processes of public life, and where a particular group marked off by color has been systematically excluded, the path to participation inevitably leads to concepts such as the development of separate power. We can see why this is so. In Mississippi the self-conscious development of the dispossessed group's power seems to be inevitable, while the group is gaining the confidence needed to break through the patterns of exclusion into which they have been pressed by long-continued prejudices.

Here the Delta Ministry is forced to walk the tightrope which history has stretched across the chasm between the races. On one side there is continued subservience for the poor if they do not learn participation in power; on the other side is future warfare between power competitors if they do not learn to move on through learned participation in power to an accepted confrontation between equals. The Delta Ministry is called to serve the process of self-determination (not being pushed back by fear of conflict). For behind the political struggle the Christian sees the deeper human struggle for the dignity of the person in God's free and open family. For this reason the Delta Ministry will need to continue to support *community organization* which allows the people themselves to develop their own leadership, state their own priorities, and press for changes to meet their needs even when this leads to conflict, controversy, and the initial pressing of their sectional claims against the groups that control power. But on the other hand the Delta Ministry is also called to serve the process of moving through conflict to *the overcoming of separation between groups.* For behind the political struggle the Christian sees that God is seeking to lead us into his open community in which there are neither black nor white, possessor nor dispossessed.

In this process of working toward political responsibility *the methods* used are themselves an issue of continuing controversy. Some would say that the Christian should limit himself to pressure within the law and by reasonable persuasion. Some insist that there are situations where the methods must go beyond this and include demonstrations and the use of a variety of pressures that break through the locally accepted patterns of action, since those who control the structures of society (often including its local political and legal processes) use those structures as essential means for maintaining unjust power patterns. To move toward justice, therefore, often requires confrontation with misused power.

Again, effective tactics cannot be spelled out in advance. Christians, knowing the reality of original sin, should not be surprised when rational persuasion proves to be inadequate to convince the possessors of power that they are using their power unjustly. For that reason the National Council of Churches has recognized the necessity on occasion for demonstrations and challenge to unjust laws. But similarly the knowledge of the reality of original sin also should lead to the recognition that the motives for challenging the laws are also likely to be ambivalent. For that reason the National Council of Churches has recognized the necessity for careful checks on participation in demonstrations. These existing guidelines need to be collected into a single document and where policy gaps exist they will need to be filled in by the Program Board of the Division of Christian Life and Mission.

4. *Educational Maturity*

We spoke of the opportunity system as including economic, political, and educational aspects. This last is pivotal; for without rapid literacy training, job training, political education, and spiritual growth, the doors of opportunity may open without the excluded being able to enter the promised land.

The Delta Ministry, again, cannot directly perform all these tasks. It can serve as an effective agent (with others) in working toward these goals. It is important here as under the other goals to suggest the several roles that the Ministry may need to play from time to time.

a) *The enabling role:* taking the initiative in stimulating concern, and helping to mobilize appropriate leadership.

b) *The participating role:* sharing with other agencies in the development of programs.

c) *The implementing role:* actually carrying out some programs, even (in unusual cases where no feasible alternative exists) with the use of federal funds.

d) *The ministering role:* standing alongside others who are implementing essential programs to help them fulfill their role.

The strategy question concerning which role or roles would be played in particular circumstances can only be decided as the situations develop in the light of available resources and in the light of potential allies.

In the Delta Ministry's work in helping to bring educational maturity to the deprived, the enormity of the task makes it essential to seek for allies in both public and private sectors in pressing towards particular program possibilities.

So far we have spoken of the major goals of the Delta Ministry *for the dispossessed.* To these could be added other allied tasks that are needed from time to time, such as legal services. And *through and behind* these particular goals which are the framework of our human existence, the church is called to bring to man's awareness *the total claim and promise of God upon our lives.* God's purpose penetrates all these realms, and for that reason we must serve men's needs in all these realms. But God's purpose overarches all these realms, and for that reason we are called to summon men to know that God's Kingdom is near and that they are invited to enter. To speak of the Kingdom without involving ourselves in the depths of human need is a mockery. To involve ourselves in those needs without maintaining an awareness of the Kingdom that stands behind them is shallowness. Our witness is not to men's need, but to Christ as the servant and savior of men in their needs.

II. Work with Other Segments of the Community

We come now to a difficult role for the churches in Mississippi. The Evaluation Committee, while stressing that the Ministry must be "essentially with the dispossessed," spoke of the need for it to be *"a Ministry also with other segments of the community (particularly with the white and middle-class Negro communities)."*

The problem of ministry to the white poor has been mentioned in the preamble. Another major issue is the relation of the Delta Ministry to the white middle-class community. In several places a strong criticism of the Delta Ministry has been that it has failed to carry out a ministry to the white people, and has failed to bring the constituency of the white churches into its confidence. Here we are in a situation of real ambivalence. What is called for in "a ministry to whites"? The dispossessed have asked for a ministry from "outside" and have welcomed it. Many *whites,* on the other hand, have resisted a ministry to the dispossessed from "outside" and have also rejected all approaches of attempted interpretation. Must it not be said that much of the white criticism of a Ministry that has concentrated on work with the dispossessed is in fact a rejection of a ministry that *is* already to them—a ministry which challenges them to question the structures of prejudice in which they too are prisoners? Unfortunately, for many, a Ministry which seeks to be with the dispossessed (especially where these primarily are Negro) and with the white middle-class at the same time is at present virtually impossible.

Does that mean that nothing more can be done? No. The privileged are not a single unvariegated group. Some do realize the need for involvement in the process of radical social change, and a real attempt must be continued to enlist them (and in various degrees, for not all can move at the same speed) in the work of the Delta Ministry. *Some may serve as members of the Commission*, provided they are willing to accept its goals and do not wish to use membership to undermine it. Others may serve in some of the *programs of the Ministry*, being ready to work on particular goals. Still others may realize the need to change some of the rigid patterns of church and social life, without yet being ready to participate in any real programs of radical social change. For these a structured path is required which will enable them to examine their past attitudes and seek to find the way to a different future. We suggest that here a *separate National Council of Churches approach* may be needed *outside the regular Delta Ministry structures*, and ask whether the Division of Christian Education may be prepared to explore the feasibility of such a ministry. We suggest also that United Church Women may be able to develop special strategies of work with women's groups working in this same direction.

III. Mt. Beulah

Finally we feel it essential to comment on the suggestion that, because of its cost, Mt. Beulah be closed. We recommend that, because of the value of the site and its present and potential uses, every attempt be made to keep it.

A decision here demands a judgment: Is the cost of Mt. Beulah incommensurate with the advantages it provides? Unless a lot more money is raised, the answer must be "yes." But we are strongly of the feeling that this would be a great loss for two reasons:

1. *Symbolically*, its closing would give great aid and comfort to opponents of integration and civil rights, for it has become an important symbol which they have insistently attacked. To close it would suggest that they can still win the big battles.

2. Mt. Beulah serves a vital purpose by being a friendly space in a still hostile environment. To it the oppressed can turn for a place to meet, to plan, and to hope. The church here gives them an oasis that speaks of a new land on the other side of the wilderness.

> Kenneth G. Neigh, Chairman, Goals Committee
> Gerald J. Jud
> James F. McRee
> Lee G. Whipple
> George A. Wiley
> Paul Moore, Jr., ex officio
> David Ramage, Jr., ex officio

Notes

INTRODUCTION

1. Tracy Sugarman, *Stranger At The Gates* (New York: Hill and Wang, 1966), Introduction, p. ix.
2. Alan Paton, *Cry, the Beloved Country* (New York: Scribner's, 1968), p. 272.

MISSISSIPPI

1. Hodding Carter, III, *Mississippi Black Paper* (New York: Random House, 1965), Introduction.
2. *Sports Illustrated*, Vol. 27, No. 11 (September 11, 1967), p. 70. (In fairness to *Sports Illustrated*, it ought to be pointed out that its five-part series in July, 1968, "The Black Athlete: A Shameful Story," is the most courageous and important series ever undertaken by a sports publication.)
Robert Sherrill, in *Gothic Politics In The Deep South* (New York: Grossman, 1968), pp. 174-5, notes the phenomenon thusly: "Equally spaced around the periphery of the rotunda of the capitol in Jackson, Mississippi, are four columns, in each of which is a niche, but there are no busts of heroes there although that is what they were intended to hold. Instead, in two of the niches are, temporarily at least, portraits of Mississippi's two Miss Americas, a tribute in chivalrous counterpoint to the rhapsody of Mississippi Supreme Court Justice Tom Brady, 'The loveliest and purest of God's creatures, the nearest thing to an angelic being that treads this terrestrial ball is a well-bred cultured southern white woman, or her blue-eyed, gold-haired little girl.' A third niche, when I was last through Jackson, was filled with a cardboard football schedule for the University of Mississippi."
3. Edward J. Pendergrass, "Analysis of Program of Delta Ministry" (April 27, 1966), p. 3. On file with the Delta Ministry, NCC, New York City.
4. Hodding Carter, III, "The Negro Exodus From the Delta Continues," *The New York Times Magazine* (March 10, 1968), p. 26.
5. Public Broadcasting Laboratory (New York: January 7, 1968), live program.
6. *I. F. Stone's Weekly*, Vol. XII, No. 42 (December 14, 1964), p. 1.
7. James W. Silver, *Mississippi: The Closed Society* (New York: Harcourt, Brace & World, Inc., 1963, 1964), p. 6.
8. Sherrill, *op. cit.*, p. 183.
9. "Hungry Children," Southern Regional Council Special Report (Atlanta: 1967), p. 6.
10. Howard Zinn, *SNCC: The New Abolitionists* (Boston: Beacon Press, 1965), pp. 257-262.

THE NIGHT OF WATCHING

1. Rep. Joseph Y. Resnick, *Congressional Record*, Vol. 112, No. 22 (February 9, 1966), p. 2648.
2. *Delta Ministry Reports* (New York City: February, 1966), p. 3. Much of the factual data in this chapter comes from comparing various documents,

many of which are on file with the Delta Ministry, NCC, New York City.
3. Mrs. Annie Devine, *Congressional Record*, Vol. 112, No. 22 (February 9, 1966), p. 2652.
4. *Washington Post* (Washington: February 1, 1966), p. 1.
5. *Memphis Commercial-Appeal* (Memphis: February 11, 1966).
6. If it is accepted that the group made the decision, then the answer to the question "Why participate?" follows naturally: in a ministry *with* and not *to* poor people, one doesn't back out when the heat is on. In terms discussed in the next chapter, *the world had set the agenda* and the DM was with the people.

   As a dramatization of incredible need and as an effective lubricant to sticky bureaucratic machinery, the Air Force Base seizure was remarkably successful. Criticism was often leveled in terms of whether the ends justified the means (which has a hollow ring in a country that can easily assimilate the destruction of a Vietnamese Ben Tre "in order to save it"). It ought to suffice that most any dying man is free to use extreme means to save his life; survival was the root and purpose of this action. And whose law is broken when 300 empty buildings stand alone while thousands live in shacks? Is property more important than life?

7. *Delta Ministry Reports, op. cit.,* p. 6.

   " 'Twas a famous victory' the Air Force won against the hundred civil rights squatters in the deactivated barracks in Greenville, Mississippi. Or was it? . . .

   There were no serious casualties . . . except the injury inflicted on the nation. The interests of the U.S. would have been far better served had someone in authority paid more attention to the plight of the suffering souls who had been obliged to vacate plantation shacks . . . The spectacle of so much brass leading this assault on the defenseless was peculiarly grotesque. Do generals and colonels have no more urgent business?" (*New York Post*, February 3, 1966).

8. *Memphis Commercial-Appeal* (Memphis: February 10, 1966).
9. *Ibid.*
10. The most popular song in fact that summer, playing constantly on radios and in Tee's Tavern near Mt. Beulah, was soul singer James Brown's "It's a Man's Man's Man's World." It states that man made the light, the boat, the train, the car, but it's worthless without a woman. "He's lost in the wilderness, He's lost in bitterness . . . without a woman or a girl." The "Ode to Billie Joe" was the most heard in the summer of 1967; it begins, "It was the third of June, another sleepy, dusty, Delta day," and identifies Choctaw Ridge and Tallahatchie Bridge.
11. Henry Aronson, John Mudd, and Marian Wright, "Proposed: A Kibbutz in Mississippi," *New South*, Vol. 21, No. 1. (Atlanta: Winter, 1966).
12. Roy Reed, *New York Times* (New York: July 25, 1966), p. 17.
13. Leon Howell, "Freedom City: Mississippi's New Community," *Christianity and Crisis*, Vol. XXVI, No. 17 (New York: October 17, 1966), p. 228.

THE FACES OF FREEDOM CITY

1. David Maxey and Paul Fusco, "Mississippi Tent City: The Strike That Failed," *Look* (March 8, 1966), pp. 26-29.

LETTING THE WORLD PROVIDE THE AGENDA

1. Nicholas Von Hoffman, *Mississippi Notebook* (New York: David White Company, 1964), p. 47.
2. Silver, *op. cit.*, p. 53.
3. Tracy Sugarman, *Stranger At The Gates* (New York: Hill and Wang, 1966), Introduction p. viii.
4. Silver, *op. cit.*, pp. 58-59.
5. Robert W. Spike, "Civil Rights Involvement: Model for Mission," No. 9 in a series of occasional papers, Detroit Industrial Mission (November, 1965), pp. 9-10.
6. Action of the General Board, NCC, USA (February 26, 1964).
7. Pendergrass, *op. cit.*, pp. 1-6. The italics are direct quotes; the rest is paraphrase.
8. Arthur Thomas, "An Open Letter to Bishop Pendergrass" (May 15, 1966), on file at NCC, USA. Italics added.
9. Hodding Carter, *So the Heffners Left McComb* (Garden City, N.Y.: Doubleday & Co., Inc., 1965), and Von Hoffman, *op. cit.*, pp. 64-78.
10. Walker Percy, *The Last Gentleman* (New York: Farrar, Straus, & Giroux, Inc., 1966), pp. 194-195.
11. Paul Moore, Jr., "Report of the Delta Ministry," to the Executive Committee of the General Board, NCC, USA (June 1, 1966). On file with NCC, USA.
12. Leon Howell, "The Delta Ministry," *Christianity and Crisis*, Vol. XXVI, No. 14 (August 8, 1966), p. 192.
13. Sandra Lloyd, "The Concept of Mission Implicit in the Work of the Commission on the Delta Ministry" (B.D. thesis, Union Theological Seminary, 1966), p. 62.
14. Paul Lehmann, *Ethics in a Christian Context* (New York: Harper & Row, 1963), p. 85.
15. "Goals for the Delta Ministry," Report to the General Board, NCC, USA (July, 1966), p. 6. (One might argue whether such separation of the two functions is really commanded. Matthew 25:40 clearly says that doing something for one in need is in fact witnessing to Christ. "Truly, I say to you, as you did it to one of the least of these my brethren, you did it to me.")
16. Gayraud Wilmore, Jr., "A Theological Analysis of Direct Action In Christian Race Relations," No. 1 in Occasional Papers on the Church and Conflict (Philadelphia: United Presbyterian Church, USA, 1965), p. 8.
17. *The Church for Others* (Geneva: WCC, 1967), p. 68.
18. *Ibid.*, p. 118.
19. Robert A. Raines, *The Secular Congregation* (New York: Harper & Row, 1968), pp. 4-5.
20. *The Church for Others, op. cit.*, p. 92.
21. *Ibid.*, p. 75.
22. Wayne C. Hartmire, Jr., "The Plight of Seasonal Farm Workers," *Witness To A Generation* (New York: Bobbs-Merrill Company, Inc., 1966), p. 175.
23. "Our Story," a working paper in the process of being revised, University Christian Movement (April, 1968), p. 2.
24. *The Church for Others, op. cit.*, pp. 118-119.
25. Solomon Gort, Jr., "The Negro Church in Mississippi: Its Potential and Dynamic In View Of Social Change," *Risk*, Vol. IV, No. 1 (1968), p. 46. Mr.

Gort says further, "When we speak of the Negro Church in Mississippi, we are talking about many denominations, but one people, a black people that share a common heritage of second-class citizenship. They are a people who have borne the yoke of oppression and have been castrated, to a great degree, of human dignity. The Negro church in Mississippi grew out of a plantation-slave system; in other words, the white plantation owner provided Negroes with a meeting place and a theology, both of which were designed to keep the Negro in subjection. For instance, if one would take a drive into the Mississippi countryside, he would see many Negro churches within a few miles, one on each plantation. And the theology of these churches has been that of the otherworldly (pie in the skybye and bye), rather than one addressed to the problems of this world. Such a theology gave the Negroes false hope (for the most part), and something to cling to, but the freedom of assembly gave them an opportunity to read the Bible which revealed the truth of the Christian Faith, for many. It also gave them an opportunity to create a sense of unity. . . .

"For the most part the church has been and still is mobile and decentralized and without economic stability. Therefore, it became necessary for the black church to develop ties with the white church. . . . For the most part . . . such a relationship has corrupted both the black and white church. The white church is corrupt because of too much power; and the black church corrupt due to the lack of power" (pp. 47-48).

OUTSIDE AGITATORS

1. Annual listings of aid given through the Division of Inter-Church Aid, Refugee and World Service, Geneva: WCC.
2. From a letter to the author, April 11, 1968.
3. Victor Ullman, "In Darkest America," *Nation*, Vol. 205, No. 6 (September 4, 1967), p. 177.
4. *Ibid.*
5. The quotes come from various minutes of the Executive and Divisional Committees of DICARWS, Geneva: WCC.
6. *Ibid.*
7. Miss Janet Lacey, "Report of a Visit to the Mississippi Delta Ministry" (London: Christian Aid, 1966), p. 3. (Enoch Powell's racial slurs in Great Britain in 1968 unfortunately proved Miss Lacey prophetic.)
8. DICARWS, *op. cit.*
9. Lesslie Newbigin, Letter to the *Presbyterian Outlook*, July 1, 1964.
10. T. Watson Street, "The Mississippi Delta Project," *Presbyterian Outlook*, Vol. 146, No. 26 (June 29, 1964), p. 7.

IN THIS CROESUS OF A NATION

1. Public Broadcasting Laboratory, *op. cit.*
2. Ralph McGill, writing in the *Atlanta Constitution*, said in July, 1968: "Small farmers, white and Negro, and the SCLC share one thing in common—a sense of outrage stemming from 'stabilization and conservation' payments to landowners for NOT growing crops.

   "SCLC's newsletter asks, for example, why Sen. James Eastland is paid $13,000 a month not to grow crops on his Mississippi plantation while a starving child gets $9.00 a month . . .

"In Georgia's Glasscock County, for example, rural and county seat leaders refused to establish a food stamp or surplus commodity foods program for the poor in their county. When the federal government, of necessity, moved in, those who resented the poor people's program reportedly parked cars in front of the distribution places to make it difficult for the poor to get commodity foods.

"Glasscock County, one of the poorest in the nation, had 13 farmers listed in the Senate hearings report. The top recipient drew $17,271 in 1967. The total for the 13 was $137,242."

3. Robert Sherrill, *op. cit.*, p. 320.
4. *Ibid.*, p. 317.
5. James K. Batten, Chicago Daily News Wire Service, Nov. 11, 1967.
6. As an illustration of our insensitivity, the Congress, worried by heavy expenditures in Vietnam, demanded a $6 billion cut in expenses in exchange for the 10 percent surtax requested by President Johnson. But in June, 1968, when the House started whacking away at antipoverty efforts, it not only did not touch the $12 billion highway construction program, but it also passed a prohibition on "freezing" highway funds by the Administration. As one person commented, the President was told to cut the budget, but when it came to highway construction where he might find some fat in the pork, he is being told to eat it, fat and all. People are starving and America makes highways a domestic priority.
7. Evaluation Committee Report, *op. cit.*, p. 5. The report also had several strong criticisms of the DM, not all of them consistent. It did criticize what it considered to be cases of poor financial judgment, flirtations with programs of racial separatism, and instances where it intensified the cleavage between poor Negroes and white-moderates and middle-class Negroes.
8. Leon Howell, *op. cit.*, p. 189.
9. "A Nation Within A Nation," *Time* (May 17, 1968), p. 30.
10. Paul Good, "Poverty in the Rural South," *New South*, Vol. 23, No. 1 (Winter, 1968), p. 4.